101 Computer Answers You Need to Know

101 Computer Answers You Need to Know

Gina Smith and Leo Laporte

Ziff-Davis Press
Emeryville, California

Copy Editors	Margo R. Hill and Stephanie Raney
Project Coordinator	Cort Day
Proofreader	Carol Burbo
Cover Illustration	Regan Honda
Cover Design	Regan Honda
Book Design	Tony Jonick
Word Processing	Howard Blechman
Page Layout	Tony Jonick
Indexer	Carol Burbo

Ziff-Davis Press books are produced on a Macintosh computer system with the following applications: Frame-Maker®, Microsoft® Word, QuarkXPress®, Adobe Illustrator®, Adobe Photoshop®, Adobe Streamline™, Ma-cLink® Plus, Aldus® FreeHand™, Collage Plus™.

If you have comments or questions or would like to receive a free catalog, call or write:
Ziff-Davis Press
5903 Christie Avenue
Emeryville, CA 94608
1-800-688-0448

ISBN 1-56276-339-3

Manufactured in the United States of America
⊕ This book is printed on paper that contains 50% total recycled fiber of which 20% is de-inked postconsumer fiber.
10 9 8 7 6 5 4 3 2 1

TABLE OF CONTENTS

Chapter 2:   Hardware Hints..........................34

Chapter 3: *Software Secrets*.......................*66*

Chapter 4: Time to Go Online! *100*

FOREWORD

Back when they were just computer industry cub reporters, I knew Gina and Leo were going places. After reading this book, though, I'm not so sure. This book was originally my idea! But they ran with it—and now they're going to be giving high-tech writers a bad name once the average person sees how easy and simple they make computers sound.

Or maybe not. Fact is, computer companies make their products just too damned complicated. I don't know how they stay in business. You think people would drive cars and make toast if they had to know how their automobiles and toasters worked? Apparently. The typical computer, peripheral, or software company thinks nothing of making people jump through endless hoops of bizarre acronyms that don't sound anything like they're spelled and looney installation routines that take hours and even days to complete. It should be more like minutes or seconds. That leaves you—a presumably innocent person with nothing better to do than spend your valuable time on one of these things—figuring how to make it all work. And unlike the business people who've been suffering with this stuff for years, it's not even part of your job.

Back on the syndicated radio show Leo and I used to do together—Gina took my place when I decided to do a show on public radio—we used to regularly get questions all the time from miserable people who were absolutely baffled! These people had no clue. A few of them were actually hopeless dummies, but the vast majority of them were just poor saps who've been suckered in by an industry that thinks its products are easy enough for anyone to buy, use, and install. What a joke. No wonder something like a third of the home PCs bought last year are rusting away in broom closets and basements.

In this book, Gina and Leo take the 101 most common computer questions from beginners and answer them in plain English. Talk about an innovation. From protecting your computer from dog and cat hair (did you know that the hair the fan sucks in melts into a nasty, sticky residue that can short out your chips), to deciding between a PC and a Mac, to advice on optimizing your system for multimedia entertainment, it's all here. How can you shop if you can't speak the lingo? How do you know that slick-looking salesperson isn't ripping you off? What do you do if you buy a lemon? And how can you be sure you even bought a lemon in the first place? Add a glossary and one of the most complete tech support guides I've ever seen, and it all adds up to the kind of no-frills tech book you'll find yourself turning to again and again. After you're done reading it, buy the *PC Magazine Buyers Guide* (edited by me) and get serious about computers.

Leo and Gina have done a killer job putting this thing together. Of the tens of thousands of calls we at "On Computers" have answered, these are the 101 best.

—John C. Dvorak

INTRODUCTION

Good Morning Class!

Okay, so you've finally decided it's time to buy a computer of your very own. Congratulations! You've got a lot of excitement ahead of you—and, we're guessing, a good bit of homework.

Few businesses are as jargon-happy as the computer business. Just looking at the computer ads gives you a taste of the mind-bending lingo computer buyers and users have to face every day. But you don't need to be an electrical engineer or even a programmer to figure out how to buy and use a personal computer. You just need some shopping smarts, a basic understanding of what a PC or Mac can do for you, and how its various components work together toward that end.

The Big Picture

Think of a computer as a sort of glorified combination electric typewriter-calculator-TV-telephone. Having trouble with that? Fair enough. Then let's take the analogy one step at a time.

Now, you remember electric typewriters, don't you? Those ancient machines were just like regular typewriters, except they used electronics to help typing go faster and ribbon changing go easier. Even more advanced electric typewriters offered a little display screen below the paper that would allow you to see a line of what you'd written—and even go back and change it—before you committed it to paper. For many, this was the first introduction to what is today known as word processing—the ability to write a document and modify it as much as you want to—fixing spelling and grammar, changing the order of sentences and paragraphs, and even rewriting the whole kit 'n' caboodle—before you ever print out a single paper copy.

But a computer is quite different and significantly more advanced than an electric typewriter or old-style word processor in several ways. For one thing, a computer has a cathode ray tube (CRT) attached to it that looks a lot like a TV screen. That lets you see what you're writing, drawing, or calculating as you do it. For another, a computer is infinitely smarter than an electric typewriter or a TV because it has a whole set of extremely powerful computer chips in it. These chips, beyond just helping you deal with writing and editing letters and memos, are math whizzes. The computer's ability to rapidly manipulate numbers is the main reason it's at the heart of so many businesses and offices. In fact, it's the computer's ability to manipulate numbers that makes possible all the applications people run on their computers—word processing, spreadsheets, games, multimedia titles for kids, reference works, drafting, drawing, and many other programs.

Finally, a computer has a whole set of devices attached and built in that allow you to store reams of files and programs inside—just as you would inside a file cabinet—and print them out on paper or view them on the screen whenever you feel like it. Many computers also include modems, communication devices that allow you to attach your computer to your home's telephone line. That makes it possible for you to send and receive information, messages, news, weather, and other data with computers owned and used by other people and companies.

A computer's ability to communicate in this way is what everyone is talking about when they refer to the "information superhighway." Already, millions of people around the country are using their computers daily to chat with others, run home businesses, create artwork, write books, articles, and letters, and inform and entertain themselves. The so-called "I-Way" may still be more like a bumpy country road than a superhighway, but it's getting bigger and better-traveled every single day.

Unfortunately for many new computer buyers and users, this business is rife with confusing acronyms and terms. No wonder buying a computer is a terrifying experience for many people: When you're shelling out a grand or more for a new appliance like a PC, you want to be sure you know exactly what you're buying and the kinds of things you're going to be using it for. And that's exactly what this book is about.

In this book, we answer the top 101 computer questions that people ask us on our radio and television programs every week. But before we do, let's explain the fundamental things you need to know about PC or Macintosh computers before you buy or use one. We'll explain—component by component—what this baffling badinage is all about.

The Computer inside Your Computer

When people say they've bought a new computer, they usually just say they've just bought a "486," or a "Pentium," or maybe they say they just purchased an "040." What they're referring to is the main brains of a PC or a Mac—a computer chip called the central processing unit, or CPU.

The CPU is the single most important component inside a computer. Without it, the computer wouldn't be a computer at all. The CPU does all the calculations inside the PC that are necessary for you to run programs, view data on the screen, print things out, or even turn it on in the first place. All the expensive circuitry, chips, devices, wires, and components on a computer are just there to support the CPU.

Now, you may already know from the ads or your friends that there are two distinct types of computers out there—PCs and Macs. Well, one of the big differences between them (there are many, as we'll soon see), is the kind of CPU they each have inside. Let's talk about that for a minute.

PCs are often called IBM-compatible PCs whether IBM makes them or not. That's because all PCs derive from the first and earliest PC, the IBM Personal Computer, which came out back in 1981.

IBM chose as its CPU a chip made by a then little-known company called Intel, a chip not-so-conveniently called the 8088. Because so many software programs were designed to run on that first PC, the more advanced PCs from IBM and other companies that followed that original model also were designed with CPUs that were Intel-compatible. That means they were capable of running any of the thousands of programs designed for the 8088 and 8086-based PCs, but they had more powerful features, too. There are plenty of books that will explain more about the history of the PC, but it will suffice to say that after the 8088 and the 8086 came the 80286, the 80386, and finally, the 486 and Pentium chips that are in wide use today. Each chip is more powerful than the one that came before— meaning it can compute more data faster, and therefore run more impressive-looking programs. That's about all you need to know about PC CPUs for the moment.

On the Mac side, a similar evolution has taken place since Steve Jobs and Steven Wozniak created the first Apple II personal computer in a northern California garage back in 1977. The current crop of Apples are all called Macintoshes, Macs for short. Instead of building Macs around Intel CPUs, Apple Computer Corporation chose CPUs from a big chip company called Motorola. Starting with the Motorola 68000, the line of chips progressed through the 68020 and the 68030 to the 68040. The newest Macintosh computers, Power Macs, are based on a chip that Motorola developed jointly with IBM and Apple, called the PowerPC. The first PowerPC chip was the 601. Before long we'll be seeing Power Macs based on the 603 and 604, too. Confused yet? Hey, that's why engineers come up with these nerdy names. Just remember that within a family of chips, the higher the number, the newer and more powerful the CPU.

In computer ads for the PC you might have noticed that the machine contains a 486DX2. Intel makes two kinds of 486 chips, the SX and the DX. The only difference is that the SX doesn't have special math circuitry for speeding up floating point calculations. Floating point arithmetic is the stuff you tried to avoid in high school involving powers of ten. You still don't need to know what it is. Most home applications don't use floating point. So unless you're calculating rocket trajectories in your spare time, you can buy an SX and save money.

Intel also makes SX2, DX2, and DX4 models. To explain what they are, we'll have to talk about something called "clock speed." You'll notice that there are some numbers attached to the 486 DX2 designation. They represent the clock speed of that particular chip, in megahertz (MHz). One megahertz is one million cycles per second. Each computer operation takes two or three cycles, sometimes more. So the 66 MHz CPU referred to in the ad can perform somewhere around 20 to 30 million instructions every second. That's pretty fast. The higher a chip's clock speed, the faster the chip.

That's why Intel decided to offer something it calls "clock-doubled" chips. The SX2 and DX2 are clock-doubled. That means that they run internally at twice the speed. The Intel 486 DX4 runs at three times the speed. (We know, it says 4, but this is the computer industry, remember?)

There's one other thing to know about clock speeds. You can't compare clock speeds from differing chip lines. A 33 MHz 386 is not nearly as fast as a 33 MHz 486. That's because the 486's more sophisticated design keeps stuff plugging along a lot faster. So the speed of the chip is both a function of its clock speed and its design.

The bottom line is: For the fastest PC or Mac, get the most recent CPU with the highest clock speed you can afford. That's the best way to make sure your computer won't be obsolete in a year or two.

Hard-Disk Hints

The first thing you need to know about hard-disk storage is also the last. You will never have enough. You could have the biggest hard-disk drive money can buy, but you will still want more. Count on it.

A hard disk is like the file cabinet in your office or the closets in your house. Here is where you can store all the files and programs you use with your computer. When program manuals talk about "saving a file," a hard disk is where it goes. Eventually, every computer user fills up all available hard-disk space—the same goes for file cabinets and closets—and you'll either have to start getting rid of stuff to make room, or buy a new hard disk and start all over again.

A hard disk is one of the few mechanical (as opposed to electronic) components in your computer, and it shows. It's far slower—many hundreds of times slower, in fact—than your computer's CPU or memory. It is also a lot less reliable. When something fails in a computer, more often than not it's that mechanically challenged hard disk that's at fault. This is why people copy, or back up, their files and programs to floppies and tape cartridges. If that hard disk fails—and they all do, sooner or later—it's going to take your data with it.

That's why it's best to have a backup copy, and why it's a good idea to avoid jostling or dropping your computers. These things are sensitive!

You can't see the hard disk unless you open up your computer's system case. It's a silvery case inside of which are several platters that look a lot like mini record albums. Your data—translated from words, numbers or images you create—gets stored on these platters in the form of 1s and 0s. Like records, hard-disk platters have tracks. To find a file, your hard disk's heads (like the needle on your record player) goes to the specific track or tracks where your file is located and reads it.

When it comes to disk storage, the basic unit of measurement is the "byte." That's because it takes one byte to represent a single letter or number. Put a thousand bytes in a row, and you've got a kilobyte. A million in a row makes a megabyte and a billion makes a gigabyte. Disk space is usually measured in megabytes, often abbreviated MB. Nerd slang for a megabyte is "a meg," as in "holy hard drive, that new word processor takes 30 megs!"

Not so long ago, a "big" hard disk could hold 20MB of information. That's enough to store the works of Shakespeare 20 times over. Sounds like a lot, right? Wrong! Today, we wouldn't recommend settling for anything less than a 340MB hard disk on PC or Mac. And if you can afford more, go for it. Hard-disk storage space is the last place you should skimp.

Finally, there's the matter of acronyms like IDE or SCSI, which often accompany the hard disk description in any ad or product description. These are simply descriptions of the technology by which the hard disk connects to the system. IDE, short for integrated drive electronics, is the preferred method for PCs. It's fast, easy to set up, and often IDE hard-disk drives plug right into your computer's main circuit board.

SCSI, short for Small Computer Systems Interface and pronounced *scuzzy*, is the preferred way to connect a hard disk to a Macintosh. All Macs have the SCSI circuitry built right in. SCSI hard disks and other SCSI devices have the unique capability of daisy-chaining—that means you can plug up to seven of them together (using the connector on the back of each SCSI device) and not have to plug each and every one of them into your computer. On the Mac, this is great news, since Macs were built from the beginning to use SCSI devices like hard disks. On the PC, it's a royal pain. It's simply untrue that SCSI hard-disk drives are faster than IDE—in fact, they're often slower—and on a PC they're quite a bit harder to install.

Flavors of Floppies

You might wonder, once you take a look at a floppy, why it's not the least bit floppy. Most floppies today are small, hard, square, plastic disks. They couldn't flop if they tried. But back in the Dark Ages of computing, floppies fit their name—they were pancake thin, black plastic disks that would just flop in the wind if you let them. So the name "floppy" just stuck. Floppies are also known as floppy disks or diskettes.

Every desktop computer comes with at least one floppy drive, a device that lets you insert and remove disks with data on them. These little disks let you save, copy, or delete files on them—either to or from your computer's internal main storage device, the hard disk. You also use disks to install new software on your computer, typically just by inserting the disk and typing a command like "install" or "setup."

These days, you hear about two kinds of floppies: 5¼-inch floppies, which are in fewer and fewer computers every year, and the more popular 3½-inch floppies. That's the size of the floppy measured across, and it's important to know. All Macs use 3½s, by the way. Many PC makers let you choose between the two—or have both—but we recommend you just get a 3½-inch drive and save the space a 5¼-inch drive would take in your computer for something a little less antiquated. Like, say, a CD-ROM drive.

Rambling about RAM

RAM is more than a male sheep; it's also one of the more macho computer acronyms you'll encounter. It also happens to be one of the most important specifications to consider when you're buying a new PC or Mac. RAM, which stands for random access memory, is just a bunch of chips the CPU uses to store information it's working on.

As we've seen, your programs and data are normally kept on the hard disk. Disk drives are reliable long-term storage devices, but they're much too slow to keep up with your speedy CPU. So the computer loads stuff from the disk drive into RAM before it works with it. RAM is fast, but forgetful. It can only hold data when the juice is on. RAM is not a permanent storage device: When you turn your computer off, everything in RAM goes away. That's why it's so important to save whatever you're doing onto your hard disk before you turn off your computer.

Most Windows and Macintosh software requires a computer with at least 4MB of memory, and more and more programs require 8MB. We don't recommend you buy any system without at least 8MB of RAM. It's always cheaper and easier to buy it now than add it later.

Stuff about Slots

One of the more comforting things about investing in a PC or Mac is the fact that you can improve a lot of its capabilities when you need to, and without buying a whole new system. That's called upgrading, and you can easily upgrade your system's sound and video capabilities or add a CD-ROM drive down the road by buying what's known as an "adapter" or "expansion" card and plugging it into one of the free slots inside your computer.

But let's talk about slots for a second. These are the longish connectors you'll see if you open up your computer case, and they allow you to plug new components into your computer. The computer industry has created an alphabet soup of standards for these slots. Naturally they're mostly incompatible with one another.

The most common slot on PCs is the industry standard architecture, or ISA (pronounced *EYE-sa*) slot. Most PCs also come with two or three "local-bus" slots. These are special high-performance connections for devices that need the speed—like graphics adapters and hard-disk controllers. We explain what local-bus slots are elsewhere in this book. All you really need to know now is that you should get a PC with ISA and local-bus slots.

It's always a good idea to get a PC with at least two free slots open—that is, with two free slots that don't already have something else plugged into them. It might sound inconceivable now, but someday the idea of popping open the PC's cover and adding new components won't make you squeamish. Well, at least not *as* squeamish.

Because Macintosh computers come with SCSI connectors and circuitry for networking, and sound and video displays built right in, Mac owners don't have as much occasion to use adapter cards. But many Macs do come with slots. There's the LC-style processor direct slot (or PDS) that's usually used for CPU upgrades, the communications slot that's used for modem or networking cards, and NuBus (pronounced *new bus*) slots that you can use for a variety of purposes. Mac owners may never use their expansion slots, but it's nice to know they're there!

Ports of Call

Ports are connectors on the back of your machine that let it communicate with the outside world.

Most PCs come with two serial ports and one parallel port. Serial ports are generally used to connect mice and modems. Sometimes you'll hear them referred to as communications ports, or comm ports. They're often labeled COM1: and COM2:.

Parallel ports are higher speed connectors used mostly for printers. That's why they're called printer ports, and labeled LPT1:, which is geekspeak for line printer one. Lately, we've seen a number of devices designed to hook up to your PC through the parallel port, including tape drives for backing up your hard disk and CD-ROM drives. Manufacturers do this because it's simpler for users to connect a device to the parallel port than it is to install an add-on card. But the parallel port connection is not very fast, so it's not the best way to expand your machine.

Some PCs also come with a game port. That's for plugging in a joystick, which is a device used to play computer games. The ports on your PC may not be labeled, but you can tell what's what because each uses a different connector.

Other connectors usually visible on the back of your PC include connections for your keyboard, monitor, loudspeakers, and microphone (if you have a sound card).

On the Macintosh, there are also a number of connectors. Apple labels these connectors with icons. There's a modem port and a printer port. The printer port can also be used to network your Mac with another machine.

Macs also come with sound connectors for speakers and microphones, SCSI connectors for adding disk drives, CD-ROMs, scanners and other devices, and a connector which Apple calls the Apple desktop bus or ADB port. The ADB port is designed so that you can attach several different devices to one connector, including a keyboard, mouse, joystick, and drawing tablet.

One of the toughest parts of setting up your new computer is figuring out what devices connect to these ports in the back.

Of Mice and Keyboards

If you plan to use your computer for anything but a night light, you'll need some input devices. The most common of these are the keyboard and the mouse.

Every personal computer ever shipped has had a keyboard, and we'll assume you have a pretty good idea what to do with one. But the mouse is a relatively recent addition. You use a mouse to control a pointer on the screen. A mouse is a very handy way to interact with the computer. It can save you a lot of typing, and can even do things it would be very hard to do with only a keyboard, like dragging pictures from one part of the page to another. Now, we've seen some people get pretty confused by mice. One fellow we've heard of tried to put it on the floor and use it as a foot pedal. Another woman tried to hold the mouse up to the screen to move the pointer. And you may remember Scotty in one of the Star Trek movies trying to use a mouse to speak with the computer. Needless to say (we hope), none of these is the proper way to use a mouse.

You roll the mouse around on top of your desk to move the arrow on the screen. Sometimes the arrow is called a pointer, sometimes it's referred to as the cursor. Macintosh mice have a single button. PC mice usually have two or three. In general, you click a button when you want to perform an action, like pushing an on-screen button, or activating a menu. The best way to learn about a mouse is to use it. If your computer comes with a mouse tutorial, we strongly suggest you take a few minutes to go through it. Knowing how to use a mouse is just as important these days as knowing how to use the keyboard.

Both the mouse and the keyboard plug into your machine. On Macs, plug the keyboard into the ADB port in back, then plug the mouse into the keyboard. On PCs, you plug both into the back. Your PC will have a dedicated keyboard port, and may have a special mouse port. If it doesn't, you'll want to use COM1: for the mouse.

One other thing worth noting about keyboards and mice: Some computer sellers will quote you a price that does not include either of these essential items. It's a form of lowballing. In the Mac world, prices often do not include keyboards or displays. If you're doing comparison shopping, check the fine print to make sure that all the machines are comparably equipped.

The Graphics Picture

Another important thing to think about—especially when you're talking about PCs—is what kind of graphics display it offers. What we're talking about here is the combination of the PC's monitor (or CRT) and the graphics circuitry inside that controls what you're seeing on the screen. The better the graphics, the faster and clearer your images will appear on screen. Graphics circuitry also governs how many colors you can see at a time on screen, which can range anywhere from 4 colors to some 16 million.

Terms that come up a lot when you're talking about graphics technology on the PC are VGA, SuperVGA, windows accelerator and local-bus. We won't bore you with the details—but here's a quick overview.

For one thing, your graphics circuitry and monitor have to match. For instance, if you have a SuperVGA monitor, you need a graphics card or circuitry inside your PC capable of generating SuperVGA images. If you're buying a PC today, we recommend you get one that offers at least SuperVGA graphics. That means you'll be able to display as many as 256 colors (most of the latest multimedia programs like that a lot), and at a high resolution that looks crisp and clean. If you're using Windows, you'll definitely want local-bus SuperVGA graphics or Windows accelerator SuperVGA circuitry inside. All VGA and SuperVGA monitors will work with these technologies, which basically serve to boost performance and limit the time you spend waiting for Windows to do things on the screen.

The good news is that most new PCs on the market offer SuperVGA graphics and sometimes even SuperVGA local-bus or video accelerator graphics built right in. Many, additionally, let you choose the size and type of monitor you get. The most common size today is 14 inches (that's measured diagonally), but if you can spring for it, get a 15- or even 17-incher. Not only is it easier on the eyes, but it will also give you more room to work on the screen. Further, monitors are adjustable—like TVs, you can adjust brightness, color, and sometimes other settings, too. Look for a monitor with controls in front to make adjustment easier. When it comes to monitors, never buy before you try. Only you know whether you'd be willing to spend hours every day staring at the thing.

Multimedia at a Glance

The hottest new trend in computing is, of course, multimedia. This is the ability to run programs with sound and animation, even video, in addition to the text, numbers, and static pictures your garden variety computer can display.

Why would you want all that? Well, for starters, maybe you want to play games. Or run educational titles for the kids. Or maybe you want to take a look at the latest multimedia reference titles that feature video and sound clips. Multimedia software is one of the fastest growing and most exciting areas in the computer industry.

Adding multimedia capabilities to your PC or Mac is just a matter of attaching a CD-ROM drive, sound circuitry, and speakers. A CD-ROM drive uses discs just like the ones your stereo's CD player uses—but instead of music, these CDs store up to 650MB worth of information. Multimedia programs need all that room to hold those huge animation, video, and sound files. Sound circuitry is required to convert digital data into something your speakers can reproduce. And don't skimp on the speakers. The better they are, the better the whole thing will sound.

If you're interested in multimedia—and most people are these days—the best thing to do is get a PC with multimedia capabilities already built in. That's because adding multimedia hardware after the fact can be a real pain. If you do choose to add a CD-ROM, sound card, and speakers to a PC you already own, make sure you get one of the all-in-one multimedia upgrade kits on the market. That way you can be guaranteed that everything will work together.

Macintosh owners, you can take it easy. The PC was designed in the days when computer sound meant making a mechanical beep that sounded like a mosquito's love call. And video meant "Leave It To Beaver" reruns on the TV. Macintosh computers, on the other hand, take to multimedia naturally. They have sound hardware already, and the built-in SCSI connecter means that adding a CD-ROM drive is as easy as plugging in a cable.

Now all you've got to do is head out and find some hot multimedia titles, and that brings us to software.

Something about Software

Every PC or Mac user needs software—whether it's for word processing, crunching numbers, doing taxes, playing games, or whatever. But that software needs a layer of technology between it and the silicon workings of your computer to communicate with it. That layer is commonly called an operating system. An operating system provides a common way for the programs to receive your input from a keyboard or mouse, and a standard way for them to store and retrieve files, print, and show information on the screen.

Most PCs come bundled with an operating system called DOS (rhymes with "toss") and a graphical environment on top of that, called Microsoft Windows. We would like to say that that's all you'll ever need to know about it, but the fact is, DOS and Windows are going to take some getting used to. If you don't know rudimentary DOS commands (such as DIR, for calling up a directory, or WIN for starting Windows) or you're not quite sure how to work with programs designed specifically to use Windows's more attractive interface and conventions, it would be a good idea to do some studying in your manual or get a tutorial-type book that will help you with the basics.

Macintosh computers, on the other hand, always have the Mac operating system (Mac OS) and an interface for using it built right in. Macs are generally considered to be easier to learn and use than PCs running DOS and Windows. Again, though, it's a good idea to get some help. There's no danger of blowing anything up, of course, but knowing a little bit ahead of time will save you a lot of time and hassle in the long run.

OK, class. You've learned the basics, now we're ready to take questions. On the following pages you'll find 101 of the questions we hear most often. If you read our answers, you'll know more about computers than 99 percent of people in the United States, including more than a few people who claim to be experts. This stuff really isn't that tough. If it were, do you think we'd see so many 10-year-old computer whizzes?

We'll try to stay away from technical terms, but if you come across a word you're not sure of, flip to the back of the book. There you'll find a complete glossary of computer jargon. And if you're up for more reading, check out the list of other Ziff-Davis Press books that we've included.

If you've still got any unanswered questions, we'd love to hear them for future editions. You can reach us via e-mail at puppyhair@aol.com. Or write to us in care of Ziff-Davis Press. We don't guarantee a personal answer, but if we use your question in the second edition, we'll be glad to send you an autographed copy.

Now on to the questions!

CHAPTER 1:
Let's Go Shopping

Spending thousands of dollars on something you don't really know that much about is definitely scary! In this section we take the fear, uncertainty, and doubt out of buying a computer. Well, we try, anyway.

1. MY SISTER HAS A MACINTOSH, AND SHE SAYS IT'S BEST FOR MY HOME. **But my brother calls her nuts, and keeps insisting that IBM PC compatibles are cheaper and more powerful. The two of them are driving me crazy! I don't mean to sound too dramatic here, but who should I believe?**

—Mixed Up in Michigan

Let's put the family feud on hold for a minute and take a look at the facts: Sure, Macs are easier to set up, learn, and use than PCs. And they are, in fact, just as capable.

On the other hand, did you know there are about nine PCs for every Mac out there? That generally means better pricing and selection on PC software and accessories. Just call it the free market at work.

So which one's best? There's really no right answer. As far as we're concerned, both Macs and PCs are just fine. But there are some factors to consider.

First, what are you planning on using this new computer for? The biggest mistake many people make when computer shopping is forgetting that it's the programs running on a computer that really count. First decide what software you want to run, then you can figure out more easily what hardware you'll need to buy.

Say you've got a PC at the office and you think you'll be taking work home. Then it makes sense to get a PC at home that will run the same software. On the other hand, if your young kids use a Mac at school, you might want one at home. Older kids might get more out of a PC, since there's a much wider selection of software (not to mention games) out there.

If you're doing lots of graphics work—retouching photos, creating artwork, editing home movies—you probably already own a Mac. Creative types naturally gravitate to it, so there is a tremendous variety of graphics and design-related Mac software available. Similarly, since PCs predominate in corporate settings, accounting, charting, and other serious business software for the PC abounds.

Choose your weapons

Again, remember that your choice— Mac or PC—really depends on the applications you run.

Your choice also depends on which system you feel more comfortable using. We suggest you spend some time with each of your siblings—for the sake of family unity, do it separately—and get a little hands-on experience with both systems. Try out their software, see how you get along with the Mac and PC, and figure out which platform suits you best. Then make the decision for yourself. Don't let your family or any other so-called experts tell you what to buy. After all, you're the one who's going to have to live with it.

TIP

Should you buy a Mac or a PC for your home? The answer depends on who will use the computer the most. Younger kids probably use a Mac at school, but older kids may prefer a PC because there are more game and software choices. But if you use a PC at work, you'll want a PC at home if you're the type who takes work home. Decide carefully.

---

2. **Is there a computer I can buy that's good for kids but that I can use, too?**

—Duncey Dad in Dallas

Always remember that when it comes to buying a computer, your kids know more than you do. After all, your kids have been growing up with this stuff. They'll have no trouble using any machine you put in front of them—it could be a Mac, a PC, or a $10,000 minicomputer. That's why, instead of asking what computer is good for your kids, you need to know what computer will be good for you. Hey, it's your money! And the answer is a lot easier than you think.

Little kids will love the newest wave in jazzy interactive storybooks. And you'll love the fact that they're spending less time zoning out in front of the TV.

In all likelihood, you need a computer that's powerful enough for word processing (writing letters and reports), home finance applications (balancing the budget), and whatever else you plan on doing with it. But your kids—and the kid in you, for that matter—want fun: killer games, multimedia rock 'n' roll, jamming animations, and whizzy video. You get the idea, right? Little kids will love the newest wave in jazzy interactive story books, funny early reading helpers, and multimedia funhouse kits. And you'll love the fact that they seem to be spending less time zoning out in front of the TV.

So, to get the best of both worlds, you need what's known as a multimedia computer, and you'll probably end up shelling out around $2,000 for it. That means a PC with at least a 486 processor running at 33 megahertz (MHz), or a Macintosh with a 68040 processor running at 25 MHz or better, 8 megabytes (MB) of RAM, a 340MB or larger hard disk, stereo sound, external speakers, and, of course, a double-speed CD-ROM drive. Don't know what it all means? Check out our handy multimedia computer shopping list on the next page. Or relax, and just ask the nearest kid.

3. **I want to set up a home office. What kind of system should I be looking for?**

—Wisconsin Workaholic

Boy, has your boss got you whipped! As if you don't already spend enough time at the office, now you want to rush out and pony up your own cash to buy a home workstation so you can lose your weekends to the job, too. Sheesh. We can only hope that this home office idea of yours is just a thinly veiled disguise for the amazing multimedia games system you're secretly planning for your den. If so, just admit it and reread our answer to the previous question.

If not, think for a minute about what kind of programs you'll be running on your home office machine. If you really are planning on bringing work home, you need a machine just like the one you've got in the office. This is great news if you're on a budget. That's because offices are usually way behind the curve in terms of giving their hard-working employees the latest in breaking technology. The typical computer in the workplace right now is a sluggish 486 PC compatible with a miserable 4MB of memory and a dinky 100MB hard disk. This is fine for word

Tools of the weekend workaholic

Take this with you when you go to the store, and look for a computer that offers at least the following features:

Multimedia/Home Computer Shopping List

CPU

➤ IBM Compatible: 486 DX2/66 or Pentium

➤ Macintosh: 68040 or PowerPC

That's the *minimum*. For the brains of your new multimedia computer, you'll want something really speedy. For maximum longevity, get the fastest CPU you can afford.

Memory

➤ 8 megabytes (MB)

This should be enough for Windows or the Macintosh. But both Macs and PCs love memory—the more you can give them, the faster they'll run.

External Processor Cache (PC Only)

➤ 256 kilobytes (K)

486 and Pentium computers use fast memory called cache RAM to speed up execution. A computer without cache is considerably slower, so make sure you have at least 256K worth.

Storage

➤ 340MB hard disk

Hard-disk space is like chocolate. Some people can never get enough. But it's cheaper to get it up front than it is to add it later.

Graphics

➤ Local bus video

Local bus is a method of connecting display cards so that the

Multimedia/Home Computer Shopping List (continued)

computer can display graphics faster. If you're going to use a graphical operating system like Windows or OS/2 Warp, you'll need that speed. For 486 systems, look for for VL-BUS capabilities. Pentium systems are better off with PCI.

Monitor

➤ 14-inch monitor

Don't go any smaller than a 14-inch monitor (measured diagonally). If you can afford it, a 17-inch monitor is infinitely easier on the eyes.

CD-ROM Drive

➤ Double speed

Almost all multimedia titles come on CD-ROM discs. They look just like audio CDs and hold 650MB of programs, pictures, video, and sound. Double-speed CD-ROM drives spin faster, so video and animation look smoother.

Sound (PC only)

➤ 16-bit stereo, Sound Blaster compatible

Macs come with sound built-in. On PCs you'll want to buy a sound card that supports CD-quality audio. That means 16-bit, stereo sound output. And since virtually all PC multimedia titles work with Creative Labs's Sound Blaster card, make sure your sound card is compatible so it'll work, too.

processing and accounting, and you can duplicate it in your very own home for around $1,000. You may also want a modem if you're interested in telecommuting or doing other business-related research online. (See Chapter 4.)

But we're betting the frugal little system we just described won't satisfy you for long. One day, you'll be slaving away in your home office on some sunny

Q/A

Saturday morning when everyone else is out playing golf. And you'll want to blow off some steam with a cool title that isn't work related at all. Maybe you'll feel like checking out one of the all-time favorite moments in sports history. Maybe you'll want to check out the latest news photos off the AP wire. Maybe you'll want to play Doom, or Mortal Kombat, or Tetris. Maybe, just maybe, you'll want to get your mind off your miserable work. And mark our words, that crummy, bargain basement box you bought is going to leave you out in the cold. That said, spring for at least a 486DX2/66 processor, with at least 8MB of RAM, a 340MB hard disk, a modem rated at least 14.4 kilobits per second, and Windows-accelerator or local bus graphics. If that's Greek to you, you're not alone. Just clip out the shopping list and take it to the store. Then ask the boss if it's okay if you spend a day or two every week working at home. After all, you're much more productive with that fast machine at home, aren't you?

> *The typical computer in the workplace right now is a sluggish 486 PC with a miserable 4MB of memory and a dinky 100MB hard disk. But we're betting that frugal little system won't satisfy you for long at home.*

4. **How important is a brand name? Is it worth paying a little more to get a computer made by a well-known company? Are there any companies I should stay away from?**

—*Baffled in Boise*

When IBM shipped its first Personal Computer in 1981, it did something unheard of in the electronic world: IBM published complete details on how to make the new machine. It was the equivalent of printing the secrets of the Manhattan Project in the *New York Times*, and IBM's revelation dropped just as big a bombshell in the computer industry. Within two years, dozens of companies were making IBM-compatible computers, and a standard was born.

Today there are hundreds of companies making PCs. Most of them use the same parts, so you can be pretty sure that, no matter who you get your computer from, it will run the wide variety of software written for the PC. Parts, as the lady on the chicken commercial used to say, is parts.

Unfortunately, there are huge differences among companies in manufacturing standards, and in the quality and availability of help they offer their customers. In general, big companies like Dell, Compaq, Gateway, DEC, AST, and, yes, IBM, offer reliable computers and high-quality technical support. But you'll pay a 10 to 25 percent premium for it.

Certainly, you can get a much better deal if you're willing to buy a PC from a small manufacturer or reseller. They have to offer better prices to compete with the big guys, and you're not paying for those huge ad campaigns featuring movie stars. But we only recommend buying a no-name PC clone if you know what you're doing, and have a lot of free time to devote to troubleshooting.

On the Apple side, things have been much simpler. Until recently, if you wanted a Macintosh you bought it from Apple. Period. And it was that lack of competition that kept the prices of the Mac so high. All that is about to change, though. Apple has finally agreed to let other companies make Mac-style computers. In the long run that should help drive prices down, but the jury's still out on how well the new Macintosh clones will perform. If past experience is any indication, you'd do well to wait a year or so to buy. (That's our rule with any new type of machine.) By then they should have all the wrinkles ironed out. Until that time, if you want a Mac, buy it from Apple.

Bottom line: If this is your first computer, buy a brand name from a reputable retailer who will offer you help and encouragement after the sale. It may cost a little more up front, but you'll save a lot of time and worry in the long run.

Bigger isn't always better, but it's likely these top computer sellers will be around for awhile.

1. Apple	**6.** Dell
2. Compaq	**7.** Gateway
3. IBM	**8.** NEC
4. Packard Bell	**9.** Acer
5. AST	**10.** ALR

---

5. **Why can't I just buy a little portable Apple Powerbook or IBM Thinkpad as my only computer? I move around a lot, and I hate being chained to a desk.**

—*Footloose in Fremont*

Who doesn't hate being deskbound? But you'd have to want to be pretty footloose, Footloose, to limit yourself to a laptop as your only computer. A seven pound or lighter notebook-sized computer is a wonderful thing, as long as you use it in addition to—and not instead of—your desktop computer.

Why? Because you'll pay the big bucks for a sleek, comfortable unit that's as usable as your desktop PC. Right now, for instance, you'll pay about $4,000 for a top-of-the line color laptop. For that price you could buy *both* a lesser laptop and a powerful desktop computer, and still have enough left over for a Greyhound ticket to Bakersfield.

If you settle for an affordable portable, costing around two grand, the bad news gets worse. For one thing, you're going to get inferior screen quality. Most laptop screens are washed out, they're all small, and many are so cheesy it's easy to lose track of the mouse pointer if you move it too fast. And those little keyboards are cramped! The key caps are so small and bizarrely laid out that touch typing can become a real pain.

> *You'll pay the big bucks for a sleek, comfortable laptop that's as usable as your big old desktop PC.*

And forget adding more sound, multimedia, and other new components down the line. Expanding these little guys isn't easy. Many portables only work with PC Cards, expensive credit card–sized devices, and they can only accommodate two of them at best.

Moreover, laptop batteries are notoriously wimpy. Divide any claims about battery life by three. When the manufacturer says you'll get six hours, expect two. And unless you take care to discharge your battery fully before you charge it, you'll notice a steady decrease in total battery life. Even though laptops can be battery powered, it's best not to leave your power cord behind.

On top of all this, your little laptop is about 60 percent more likely to fail than a comparable PC or Mac desktop machine. After all, it takes a lot more abuse. Life's not easy for a laptop that you toss into your luggage, dump in your trunk, or drop a few times a month. Laptops are also more susceptible to heat disasters— those cramped cases don't leave much room for heat to dissipate, and sometimes your chips get fried.

You wouldn't want to replace your PC or Mac with a notebook computer, but if you've got the bucks to have one as your second computer, go for it! Look for these key notebook computer features.

Notebook Computer Shopping List

Weight

➤ Seven pounds or lighter

It doesn't sound like a lot, but anything heavier will weigh you down with major back and neck pain in a hurry. And the weight, including the power supply, definitely shouldn't exceed 8.5 pounds.

CPU

➤ 486DX2/50 or faster

Again, the more power you can afford, the better.

Memory

➤ 8MB RAM

You'll need at least this much if you plan on running Windows applications.

Hard Disk

➤ 340MB RAM

There's nothing worse than sitting in an airport somewhere desperately deleting files so that you can save your data before the battery runs out. Also, definitely get a notebook that has a floppy drive.

Batteries

➤ NIMH or lithium ion

Try to buy a notebook that offers nickel hydride or lithium ion batteries. They don't wear out as fast.

Notebook Computer Shopping List (continued)

Display

➤ Backlit active matrix or dual-scan passive matrix display

All laptops use liquid crystal displays (LCDs), and an active matrix LCD is top of the line. It will look every bit as good as your desktop monitor—maybe better—but active matrix is expensive, as much as $1,500 for the screen alone. Passive matrix designs tend to look a little washed out. But the newer dual-scan passive matrix screens are a good compromise between price and performance. Take a look at the screen you plan to buy in a variety of lighting. And make sure the screen is backlit for those situations where there's no light at all. Hey, you never know.

Pointer

➤ Integrated pointing device

Think about it. Where are you going to put the mouse when you're contorted in some dinky plane seat? The best notebook computers offer a built-in pointing device or trackball. Definitely try out the pointing device before you buy to see if you can get used to it.

Key size

➤ 18 millimeters or larger

Anything smaller than this will make you want to tape toothpicks to your knuckles! The standard size for a regular keyboard key is 19mm—try to get as close to standard size as you can. And make sure you can live with the key layout. The arrow keys, in particular, are often oddly or illogically placed.

Security

➤ Password protection

If you'll be carrying around sensitive information on your notebook, think about getting one with password protection. Password-protected PCs are not invincible, but they'll keep the casual crook from ransacking your hard drive.

Still reading? Well, if you really think you're careful enough—not to mention rich and carefree enough—to have a laptop as your sole computer, definitely try before you buy. Make it a rule. Read all the reviews you can get your hands on to narrow the selection to two or three top contenders, then shop 'til you drop. Bang on the keyboard. Stare at the screen. Spend as much time as you possibly can getting a feel for whether or not you could live with that new machine. Maybe its particular little keys and cramped screen will drive you crazy.

Look at durability testing data, too. Is the hard disk or internal circuitry "shock-mounted" to protect it in minor bumps and falls? What about the warranty? You'll want at least a one-year parts and labor warranty for one of these babies.

Every laptop is a give-and-take proposition—you'll sacrifice some features to gain others. Considering the prices they're getting for these slimline wonders, don't jump into any laptop purchase without a lot of thinking first.

6. **My friends make fun of me because their PCs have "Intel Inside" stickers on the front and mine doesn't. Does it matter that my PC doesn't have an Intel Inside sticker?**

—Ostracized in Ohio

Your friends are absolutely, positively 100 percent wrong. There. Feel better? That five cent plastic decal is hardly a guarantee of quality. Even though it might look that way, the Intel Inside label isn't a seal of approval, not even close.

> *Don't be ashamed if you don't have an Intel-Inside sticker on your PC, or even if the model you bought doesn't have an Intel-made CPU at all. You'll still be able to do all the same things as your friends.*

For computer makers, though, it means a lot. You see, Intel makes the microprocessor that powers most, but not all, IBM-compatible PCs. A couple of years ago they came up with this ingenious marketing scheme to build brandname recognition. When a PC maker like Compaq or Dell puts the Intel Inside logo on its box, Intel helps them pay their advertising bills. And consumers get the impression that buying a PC built around an Intel 486 or Pentium CPU is the only way to go. We hope the genius who came up with this one has retired wealthy by now.

One of the reasons Intel started this advertising campaign is that it's facing growing competition from companies like AMD, NexGen, and Cyrix, which are making Intel-compatible, PC-compatible microprocessor chips. New PCs built around these so-called "clone" chips are either faster or cheaper—or faster *and* cheaper—than Intel-based computers, but they still run all the same DOS, Windows, and OS/2-based software. That's why many reputable computer makers—including Compaq and IBM—have broken years of tradition and now offer clone-based PCs.

So don't be ashamed if you don't have an Intel Inside sticker on your PC, or even if you don't have an Intel microprocessor at all. You'll still be able to do exactly the same things.

7. What's the difference between a 386, 486, and a Pentium? I know about the price differences, but which one is best for me?

—Not an Engineer in Naples

The 386, 486, and Pentium are simply names for various Intel microprocessors that act as the central processing unit, or CPU, in most IBM-compatible PCs. There's a CPU at the heart of every computer—in fact, it's where all the real computing goes on in a computer. After the CPU, all those other chips, wires, and components are just gravy. Apple's Macs are typically based on Motorola's 68000 series and PowerPC CPUs.

The difference is power. All things being equal, a system based on a 33MHz 386 chip is about half as fast as a 33MHz 486 chip. Similarly, a 66MHz 486 is about

Under a microscope, a CPU chip resembles Miami

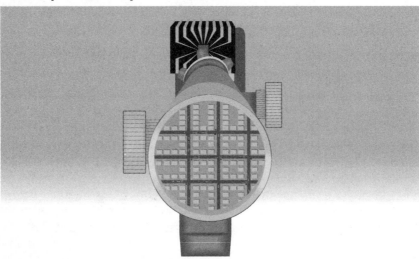

half as fast as a 66MHz Pentium. As always, we think you should buy the fastest system you can afford. Though few vendors ship 386-based systems any longer, you can pick one up in the used PC market for well under $800. That's a fast enough system for DOS-based (not Windows-based) word processing, spreadsheets, and online activities. Top-of-the-line 486 systems, fully configured, can cost you anywhere from $1,000 to $3,000. They're the absolute minimum if you're running lots of Windows programs or multimedia, games, and kids' educational programs. For state-of-the-art Pentiums, add another $1,000 to both sides of that range.

8. I'm a little confused by all the different Macintosh models. Is there a simple way to know which is which?

—*Macfreaked in Madison*

Not if Apple can help it. In recent years, it seems as if Apple's been going out of its way to come up with an incredibly confusing array of product lines.

It wasn't always so. In the early days, Apple was quite the innovator, giving its computers personable names like Lisa (Apple founder Steve Jobs's daughter's name) and Macintosh (his favorite fruit). But eventually the faceless, gray corporate mind-set invaded Apple's corridors, too, and Apple's computers began to assume names like the Centris 610, the Performa 575, and the Power Mac 8100/80. Maybe Apple figured people would respect it more if it had nerdier names for its boxes. If you're thinking of buying a Mac, be sure to scan the Mac magazines for model types and prices.

In the meantime, check out the overview below.

9. Is it OK to buy a used PC? Where's the best place to find one? How can I tell what kind of condition it's in?

—*California Cheapskate*

Buying a used PC is a great way to save money, as long as you're not the type that drools over the latest and greatest software.

Would you believe computers depreciate even faster than cars? Most computers lose 50 percent of their value within a couple of years. A five-year-old computer is worth next to nothing in resale value. Yet that same five-year-old computer is nowhere near worn out. The electronic circuitry is probably good for another 100 years. And even the parts that wear, like the disk drives and power supply, should be good for at least a few more years.

The problem with an old computer isn't that it runs out of steam. It's every bit as useful as it was on the day it shipped. It's just that you won't be able to run any new programs on it, and computer buyers are always pining for the latest software.

Q/A

If you're buying a used computer, make sure it comes with all the software you need, or that you have a reliable source of discontinued programs.

Progress in the computer industry happens so fast that two or three years can be a lifetime.

Progress in the computer industry happens so fast that two or three years can be a lifetime. Every 18 months computer chips double in power. And software designers take advantage of that fact by writing bigger, more complicated programs. That usually means you won't be able to run the next generation of software on hardware from generations past. But all the programs written for that old PC should work just fine. Often they run much faster than today's bloated software. In fact, one of us, we won't say which one, still prefers her old DOS-based word processor running on a 286 PC to a state-of-the-art Windows word processor running on a Pentium 90. Old habits die even harder than old PCs.

MAKING SENSE OF ALL THOSE MACS

The way Apple's been discontinuing some models and renaming others, it's tough to keep track of all the models of Macs there are. As of this writing the Apple product line features LC, Performa, Quadra, Power Mac, and Powerbook models. Here's how they stack up.

➤ The LC is Apple's low-end Macintosh line, intended for the primary and secondary school market. These machines have been around awhile.

➤ The Performa is the Mac that Apple especially designed for beginning and novice home buyers. For the most part, you'll find them in electronics stores and warehouse clubs, and most of them come with the multimedia components for playing CD-ROM titles built right in.

➤ The Quadra is the business Mac. It's sold through computer stores.

➤ The Power Mac is Apple's high-end line based on the new PowerPC microprocessor. Power Macs are intended for power users. Most of us don't need all that speed.

➤ All Macintosh laptops are called Powerbooks. PowerBook "Duos" are specially made portables.

Buying a used computer is like buying a used car—you can get a great deal, but you risk being taken for a ride. And just like a used car, you'll get the best deal buying direct from the seller. He or she may even throw in all their old software, too. As we've seen, that's a real plus. But we only recommend buying direct for people who know what they're doing.

If you're new to computers, and you really can't afford to buy a new machine, find a dealer who sells used equipment. You'll pay slightly more, but you'll also have someone to turn to if the computer doesn't work just right. And never buy a machine as is. Make sure there's at least a three-month warranty. A computer that doesn't work quite right will end up costing you much more in the long run.

No matter who you buy from, there are some things to watch out for. Look for disk drives that are worn or out of alignment. These drives will have trouble reading diskettes created on other machines. Older monitors sometimes have ghostly images burned into the phosphors, or they may have lost some of their brightness. Old hard-disk drives are sometimes flaky. You'll want to check them with a disk diagnostic program that can test for reliability. In general, it's best to buy the latest model you can afford. Not only will it be in better shape, but you'll be more likely to be able to find compatible software and replacement parts.

Simple? Sure. But don't get too cocky until you get a load of the confusing part. Time to take notes.

➤ **The Macintosh LC 475 is essentially the same as the Quadra 605, which used to be the Centris 605. The LC 630 and the Quadra 630 are the same except the LC doesn't have a math coprocessor. That's a specialized chip used for doing arithmetic on fractional numbers. The Quadra 630 comes in several flavors, including the 630/CD, the 637 Money Magazine edition, and the 638.**

➤ **Performas come in 400s, 500s, and 600s. In general, the larger the number, the faster the machine. Except for the Performa 570 and 630 which have the same microprocessor, but are configured differently.**

➤ **The newest Powerbooks are the 500 series.**

We could go on, but it only gets worse. And most of it would probably be out of date by the time you read this. Fortunately, there's a good rule of thumb for buying a Macintosh. Set your budget first, then buy the most Macintosh that fits your budget. In the Mac world at least, there's a pretty good correspondence between price and performance. The more you pay, the more powerful your machine. So get the most machine you can afford. With any luck, you won't start wanting a faster machine until after the kids are out of college.

10. I'm ready to buy my first computer, but where should I go? Mail order prices seem lower, but won't I get better support from a local computer store? And what about stores like Kmart?

—Saskatchewan Shopper

Yep, mail order prices are better. That's because mail order companies don't have the overhead of fancy showrooms and smarmy computer salespeople. And, despite what you may have heard, mail order vendors do offer excellent service and support. When you're buying hardware sight unseen, it'd better be. These companies build their reputations on sterling service and support. Otherwise, you'd be crazy to risk your dollars on their products.

So if you know exactly what type of PC or Mac you're looking for, buying from a reputable mail order company like Dell, Gateway, or MacWarehouse makes sense. It's likely you'll save money (check a mail order magazine like *Computer Shopper* or *MacUser* for many other big brands and price comparisons), and you'll get decent support to boot. Make sure the firm offers prepaid overnight pickup and delivery on returns in case you can't get the system working once you take it out of the box. Also—and this is true for all shopping channels—look for round-the-clock technical support. You should be able to reach a live person via a toll-free number any time of the day or night. Problems don't happen only between 9 and 5, you know.

Of course, you might feel more comfortable looking at and playing with the PC or Mac you're about to buy, and who can blame you? After all, we're talking some real money here. If that's the case, be sure to check out several stores in your area, including warehouse stores like Price Club, mass merchants like Kmart and Walmart, electronics stores like Circuit City, and computer stores like CompUSA. They'll offer very competitive prices—often comparable to mail order prices—and many use price-matching guarantees that could shave as much as $100 off your final price. And since you're paying extra for the staff, be sure to give them a real hard time by dickering over price. It might not help, but it sure can't hurt.

TIP

If you're purchasing a computer through a mail order firm, choose a company that offers these two features: prepaid overnight shipping on returns and 24-hour technical support.

---

11. **How do I know if my computer salesperson is trustworthy when I don't understand a word he says?**

—Skeptical in Seattle

What's the difference between a computer salesperson and a car salesperson? The car salesperson knows he's ripping you off! (Rimshot please.)

The computer salespeople we know really hate this joke. And you should see the mail we get from car salespeople! Most computer salespeople are professionals who know what they're talking about and take their responsibilities seriously. But even they acknowledge that there are plenty of folks selling computers who can't tell a mouse from a modem. And if you're not sure of what you're buying, scary salespeople like these can really take you for a ride.

The good news is that it's possible for you to defend against all those double-talking and nefarious computer shills out there. The key, you see, is research. Say you're buying a 486 computer and you don't want to spend more than $1,800. Then run, don't walk, to your neighborhood library and dig up every product review you can find in magazines like *PC Magazine, Computer Shopper, PC World, Home PC,* and *Family PC.*

If you're spending $1,800 or less on a 486 computer, run, don't walk, to your neighborhood library and dig up every product review you can find. You need artillery.

The idea is to get an idea of what makes and models are consistently rated highest, and to know enough ahead of time about the models you're shopping for so you can *spot* a weak salesperson. When you do find a salesperson who knows what he is talking about, and is willing to spend some time with you explaining all this stuff, hold on to him. It's a rare find.

12. **What kind of warranty should I look for? Is a one-year guarantee enough? Should I pay extra for on-site support?**

—Querulous in Québec

Here's some depressing news: Your shiny new computer—the one you spent all that money for, the one that holds your letters, banking records, work projects, everything—*will* stop working. And this will happen at the absolute worst time. Our computers usually give up the ghost about an hour before deadline, and about half an hour after the local computer store has closed. So no matter how experienced you are, and no matter how well connected, make sure you get a great warranty from the get-go.

One-year parts and service warranties have become very common in the computer industry, so there's no reason to settle for less. If the computer comes with an even longer warranty, go for it. A lot of computer buyers even make the length and type of warranty the deciding factor.

13. **I'm not sure I have what it takes to use a computer. What happens if I can't figure it out?**

—Jittery in Jasper

They say that there are 30 million home computers in the United States. What they don't mention is that about half of them are collecting dust in the bottom of closets everywhere. A great many people buy computers and then end up using them about as much as that dusty old exercise bike in the garage. Thanks to advances in power, functionality, and ease of use, this is becoming less common, but it still happens. It could even happen to you. So before you buy, you should examine your reasons for bringing home a computer.

If you've never used a computer, or you're just buying one because it seems like the thing to do, you may be making a costly mistake. A computer is not like a TV. You can't just turn it on and let it entertain you. It takes a real investment in time to learn, use, and maintain a computer. You may find it incredibly challenging and even frustrating at first. No matter what the computer industry would like you to believe, computers are a lot harder to use than the average home appliance. If you still haven't figured out how to program your VCR—or you just don't really have anything compelling to give your computer to do—think twice about inviting a computer into your life. Instead, buy a juicer or a breadmaker or something.

On the other hand, there are many excellent reasons for buying a home computer. Kids for one. Our kids are growing up in a world where computers

---

SWEATING IT OUT!

The solid state circuitry in computers is very reliable. If a chip is going to fail it tends to do so in the first few months. That's why the best manufacturers smoke out potential failures by "burning in" their computers before selling them: they leave them running for a day or two in a hot room. Computer chips fail faster when they're hot, so a computer that can sweat out the burn-in period will be more reliable. It's a good idea to look for a company or computer store that burns in its computers before sending them out.

are omnipresent. Their success in the job market may well depend on their computer skills, so there's no reason not to give them a head start. Having kids around also helps because they've got the time and motivation to learn how to use that $2,000 hunk of silicon, and maybe they'll reward you for buying it by showing you how to use it.

Another common reason to buy a computer is to bring work home. If you're already using a computer at work, your chances of successfully using a home computer are much greater. At least you'll know what you're up against.

If you don't really have anything specific you want to do with your computer, think twice about bringing one into your life. A big chunk of the PCs sold today are molding over in closets everywhere.

People often buy computers with the best intentions. They plan to organize their finances, keep track of their possessions, or even write the Great American Novel, but the vast majority of home computers are used for two things: entertainment and socializing online. So if the idea of playing cool games, or surfing the Internet doesn't appeal to you, maybe you'd be better off buying a TV instead of a computer.

Now, if after all that you still want to take the leap, go for it. A personal computer is the most wonderful toy—and tool—ever invented. With a small investment in time, you can do your taxes, balance your checkbook, become immersed in magical worlds, take down an alien or two, even write the Great American Novel. Just remember that it's going to take some time and effort to figure it all out, but we think it's well worth it.

On-site service is the house call of the computer industry. It's a nice luxury if you can afford it, but most people settle for carry-in service with a one-day turnaround. Ask for a "loaner"—a computer they'll loan you while they repair yours—if it's going to take longer than 24 hours to fix your computer.

One-day turnaround is pretty standard in the mail order biz too. The mail order company should pay for overnight postage for at least the first 90 days.

Q/A

14. I think I bought a lemon. It just won't work right, and the store can't seem to fix it no matter how many times I bring it in. Now what do I do?

—Bummed in Boulder

Hey, it happens. You get a new computer, take it out of the box, spend half an hour putting the thing together, and then boom. It's dead. Or maybe it's just dying. Maybe it won't turn on, or maybe you're just getting error messages and funny noises out of it. Welcome to every computer buyer's nightmare. Well, at least you'll have a hair-raising story to tell your grandkids.

So far there are no lemon laws to protect computer buyers, but if you've followed our advice you've purchased your computer from a reputable company that stands behind its machines, so it should be easy to take it back.

First thing, gather all the sales receipts, documentation, and other related materials and head back to the store. If you bought mail order, call the 800 number in the manual. Be sure you can describe, concisely, how your computer is acting. Does it make noise but nothing shows up on the monitor? Are there any error messages? Write them down. The more specific you are about your problem, the more likely you'll be able to get help. Tech support people hate nothing more than the call that starts, "Hey, my computer doesn't work! What's wrong?" And you'll hate racking up the minutes on the phone while they're making you put all that stuff together.

If you can't get the computer working with a single phone call or visit, the company should offer to exchange the entire computer. This is the best solution, and the one you should push for. Who needs to schlep that big box back and forth as the company tries fixing it one part at a time. Let them swap out pieces on their own time. We've heard so many horror stories of hours spent on the phone and months spent trying to find the offending part. This is not a good use of your time. When a machine won't work, exchange it!

If the seller is giving you a hard time about exchanging the machine, be persistent. Also, be nice. You catch more flies with honey, as the old saying goes, and being nasty isn't going to get you anywhere. If the salesperson still refuses to return your money, then it's time to call in the consumer watchdogs.

Most states have an Office of Consumer Protection you can call at this point. You should be able to find the number in the government section of your phonebook, or by calling 1-800-555-1212. Get on the horn with someone there, and inform them that you want to write a letter of complaint. Ask specifically what the state requires you to include in that letter. Usually, you need to get these letters into the agency within 30 days of the purchase.

(It's not a bad idea to call your local computer radio show or newspaper columnist, either. We've had a lot of fun chasing evil computer vendors on our radio shows, and often with excellent results!)

Next, you want to send a copy of that letter to your area's Better Business Bureau, the one to which your offensive retailer belongs. Don't forget to notify the store that you're sending the BBB a letter. Sometimes this alone is persuasion enough to get them to settle with you.

If you can't get the computer working with a single phone call or visit, the company should offer to exchange the entire computer. If they don't, ask them.

For any credit purchase, it always pays to know your credit card's return policies. Yes, the Federal Trade Commission has laws to protect you from getting incorrect charges on your statement. But they have limits: The purchase has to be within 100 miles of your home address. You also may need to prove you tried to resolve this problem with the seller by phone, letter, or fax. Fortunately, many credit card companies have refund policies that are much broader than this, and ones that specifically mention mail order purchases. It's always wise to know these policies ahead of time.

If the mail order computer you bought was a lemon, there are laws to protect you too. If you're shopping through the mail, online, or via fax, the law says the company *must* send you the product within 30 days or give you a delivery date. If it doesn't arrive by that specified date, you have the option to cancel the order. And if it misses any of the above ship dates and you choose to cancel, the mail order company by law must credit your account within *one* billing cycle.

There. Feel better? It pays to know your rights.

15. **I'm just going to use this computer for simple things like word processing and paying the bills. How much disk storage do I need?**

—Stumped about Storage in Stoughton

Ladies and gentlemen of Stoughton (and, yes, the world), we now give you Smith and Laporte's Law of Diminishing Disk Space: No matter how much disk space you have, you will use up 80 percent of it in the first year of ownership. We're not kidding. You'll soon see for yourself that this is true whether you have a 200MB or 2,000MB hard-disk drive. Your data will always swell to fill all available space.

So, given Smith and Laporte's Law, can you ever have enough disk space? Sorry, no. That's why it pays to start with a goodly amount, since it's considerably more expensive to add space later. For your home computer a 340MB hard drive is a great start. If you buy as much hard-disk space as you can afford when you buy that computer, your life will be immeasurably easier later. There are few things worse than having to scour your hard disk for old files to delete when you're trying to install some cool new program.

Still, it makes sense to keep things running smoothly by moving old and unused files off the hard drive onto floppy disks. Also, big devourers of disk space should check out data compression products like Stacker or Microsoft's DriveSpace. Such software can compress the files on your hard disk so they take half as much space, effectively doubling the available amount of storage on your hard disk. It's not right for everybody though.

16. I want to run Windows, but I have a question. The box says I need DOS and 4MB of RAM. Here's my question: Huh?

—Clueless in Cupertino

By now, you've undoubtedly noticed that the computer industry is rife with acronyms. Sometimes it seems like a plot to keep the rest of us in the dark. In fact, it probably is. At any rate, once you learn what all these abbreviations mean, you too can pass yourself off as a computer expert. Even if you're like most people who bandy these terms around and don't always know exactly what you're saying.

Let's start with DOS, then. This is short for *Disk Operating System*. Which brings us to the over-extended metaphor portion of our program. Try to think of your computer as a modern high rise. Each floor is occupied by a different piece of software, busy at work handling your data processing needs. The programs and files you look at are on the top floor. The silicon innards of your system are at the very bottom. Think of DOS as building management.

Every computer needs an operating system to run things. In the case of most IBM compatibles, that operating system is DOS. Most computers run Microsoft DOS, MS-DOS for short. IBM and Novell sell versions called IBM-DOS and Novell DOS. IBM also sells a more sophisticated operating system it calls OS/2. Even if you plan on using Windows, you'll need to have one of these operating systems running as well. (Towards the end of 1995, Microsoft plans to release a version of Windows, called Windows 95, that doesn't require DOS.)

Windows also requires 4MB of RAM. We've used that term already in this book. RAM, short for Random Access Memory, means the memory chips in your computer that store the applications and data you're dealing with when you're working on the computer. (When you turn the computer off, though, everything in RAM goes away. That's why you always need to "save" your documents onto the hard disk. If this is news to you, turn back to the Introduction.) At any rate, the box is right that 4MB is a minimum. But trying to run Windows with just 4MB of RAM is like trying to drive a car with the emergency brake on. You can do it, but it's slow. Windows really needs 8MB of RAM or more to keep you from forever staring at the screen, waiting for applications to pop up or pictures to display. Do yourself a favor, don't even consider buying a PC with less RAM.

17. I'm going to use this machine for games, so I want sound. There seems to be quite a range of prices. What do I get if I spend more?

—Silent in Sioux City

If you're just going to be playing games, not much. You only need a card that's labeled as 100-percent compatible with the so-called Sound Blaster standard. Most games these days require it. The Sound Blaster method of playing computerized sounds is optimized for beeps, bonks, crashes, and screams—ideal for the computer game world. For more sophisticated games, you might find it worthwhile spending a little extra for a "wave-table" version of a sound card—this is a feature that allows games supporting MIDI sound to play more realistic sounding music, scores, and effects. Once you've heard it, you'll never go back. At any rate, you shouldn't pay more than $200 for a top-of-the-line model. For a plain old Sound Blaster-type card, $100 is more like it. So be silent no more!

Many games now play in stereo... and there's nothing like hearing the scream of an F16 fighter roaring left to right.

As we've mentioned before, Macintosh computers come with sound built right in. So you Mac buyers out there are already covered.

Sound Card Shopping List

Must have

➤ Sound-Blaster compatible

➤ 16 bit-stero playback

Nice but not necessary

➤ Wave-table synthesis

➤ Software configurable

Additional special features

➤ MIDI in

MORE ON SOUND

➤ Generally the price of the sound card reflects how well it reproduces sound.

➤ Yesterday's 8-bit sound cards are incapable of high-quality sound reproduction. Even though most titles support them, we don't recommend them. On the other hand, 16-bit cards can sound every bit as good as your audio CD player. Don't settle for less.

➤ Also, make sure the card supports stereo sound. Many multimedia titles are in stereo—and hearing that F16 fighter scream from left to right sure makes a difference.

➤ Less expensive sound cards use something called FM synthesis to create these sounds. FM synthesis produces less than lifelike results. Better soundcards use wave-table synthesis. They create sounds based on digitized samples of real musical instruments. Since synthesized sound is most often used to create music, you'll get much more realistic music if you have a card that supports wave table synthesis. If you want to make music with your machine, spend the money. You'll be much happier.

➤ Higher quality sound cards may have other convenience features. To install a sound card into an existing system you'll have to set several parameters including IRQ number, DMA channel, and I/O address. Cheaper cards require you to set switches on the card. The better cards can change these parameters using just software. Look for that feature.

➤ If you'd like to play audio CDs through your system, your sound card should have an internal audio connector that attaches to the Audio Out port of our CD-ROM drive. If you want to connect a CD-ROM drive to your system, too, then you might want to find a card that supports CD-ROMs, too.

➤ Last, but not least, make sure to buy a card that's 100 percent Sound Blaster compatible. The Sound Blaster sound card from Creative Labs is so prevalent that virtually all multimedia titles support it. If you get a card that doesn't adhere to that de facto standard, there's a good chance that it won't work with some software. As usual, with computers it's better to go with the flow than to swim upstream.

18. I'd like to upgrade my 486 with multimedia components. I've heard this is really tough. Would I be better off getting a whole new system?

—Multimanic in Madison

Well, it's true that upgrading your PC with CD-ROM and sound capabilities for running multimedia can be the toughest upgrade you'll ever make. The problem is that the PC you bought was not originally designed with sound and CD-ROM peripherals in mind. So you'll end up with interrupt conflicts, a problem that occurs when more than one computer peripheral tries to communicate with the computer's CPU at the same time. Interrupt conflicts can be tough to resolve, and unless you have unlimited time and patience, we suggest you let someone else do the installation. No wonder many PC owners make the store do the upgrade for them.

That said, there are several ways to add multimedia to your existing PC. But first, you'll want to make sure your PC meets at least Microsoft's Multimedia PC Level II standard. All the latest multimedia titles you'll want to run on your PC expect a MPCII computer. A MPC Level II system starts with at least a 486SX25 CPU, 4MB of RAM (we recommend 8MB), a 160MB hard disk, and a 640×480 resolution screen that can support at least 65,000 colors. Got that? Then you can complete your multimedia configuration with a double-speed CD-ROM drive, a 16-bit sound card and a nifty set of self-powered and amplified computer speakers. And there are several different ways to skin that cat.

Really macho computer nerds prefer to buy and assemble their new multimedia components piece by piece. Are they ever asking for trouble! Making disparate devices work with your PC is the toughest route you could possibly take—not only do you have to worry about making them work with your PC, but you also have to pray that you can get the new pieces working with each other. That's why we suggest that instead you buy an all-in-one multimedia upgrade kit, one that includes CD-ROM, sound, and speakers all preconfigured to work with each other right out of the box. That way, you can just concentrate on making them work with your PC.

TIP

The easiest way to upgrade your computer with multimedia components is to buy an all-in-one multimedia upgrade kit. All the pieces in the kit—sound, CD-ROM, speakers—are pre-configured so that they'll work with one another.

So whose kit should you buy? Time to go comparison shopping again. Many companies sell what's known as multimedia upgrade kits. If you're going to be playing a lot of games and off-the-shelf multimedia titles, we recommend you get a kit that's clearly labeled "100-percent Sound Blaster Compatible." The Sound Blaster standard for playing sound is the most common one in use today. Basically, it's a method of imitating sound effects (whirs, whizzes, booms, and bangs) and musical scores (imitations of every instrument in an orchestra) to enhance game play. Sound Blaster's creator, Creative Labs, has its own line of multimedia upgrade kits in fact. But there are several other proven companies— Aztech, MediaVision, Orchid, and Reveal among them—that offer kits just as able to play games that require Sound Blaster compatibility.

Sound Blaster, then, is the key word to look for if you think you'll be running games and kids titles. Unlike the Intel Inside label, the "100-percent Sound Blaster" claim is one that sound card makers have to actually pay for and comply with. Multimedia upgrade kits start at around $300. If you buy a kit that comes with a bunch of CD-ROM titles, you'll pay more. Make sure they're titles you would actually buy.

On the other hand, if you think you'll be using your multimedia setup as a music recording studio, you'll need something better. And if you're a musician, you already know the MIDI buzzword—it stands for Musical Instrument Digital Interface. This was invented for all the hip musicians back in the late 1970s who wanted to hook up their electric keyboards, drums, and guitars to computers and do weird things.

Even though most low-cost sound cards do have MIDI chips on them, they only have enough MIDI to let you play games that have realistic, instrumental MIDI sounds. To record and mix music in stereo, you're going to need at least a sound card capable of full MIDI sampling and editing. Turtle Beach, Roland, and others sell high-end multimedia kits that offer sophisticated music-mixing features. It costs extra—starting at over $399 a card—but you'll know it if you need it.

HOW SOUND IS DIGITIZED

PC buyers have a huge selection of sound cards to choose from. All of them do the same thing, convert digital representations of sound into the analog waves your amplifier and speakers can reproduce. Cards that record do the same thing in reverse, that is, convert sound into a digital form a computer can understand.

Computers represent all data as ones and zeros, and that includes sound. Sound is "digitized" using a technique called sampling. Each sample is a picture

Q/A

19. The computer I'm looking at has a 14-inch monitor. That seems awfully small considering I have a 21-inch TV. What's the right size for a monitor?

—Up the Creek in Utica

Fourteen inches is enough for anyone. Seriously. You could get a 21-inch computer monitor, but it would cost several thousand dollars. That's probably much more than your whole computer system will cost. And it's certainly much more than your 21-inch TV set. TVs and monitors, despite their external similarities, are very different animals.

With the right components, you can even watch CNN or "All My Children" in a little window, and do it while you're pounding out your latest memo. Talk about inspiration!

Your TV set is capable of displaying 400 vertical lines. Broadcast television never uses more than 350 lines from top to bottom. On the other hand, your 14-inch monitor needs to display at least 480 lines vertically, and 640 dots horizontally to give you the crisp text and clean graphics you expect. In fact, several companies have created a good little business putting TV on your computer. With the right adapter card you can watch CNN or even "All My Children" as you pound out your latest memo. TVs are great at displaying full-motion video that comes down the cable, but don't try to do word processing on them!

For most applications, 14 inches is more than sufficient. If you'd like to see a full page of text in your word processor you might want to buy a bigger monitor. Especially if you're doing really detailed graphics work in desktop publishing, illustrations, or photoediting. Seventeen-inch monitors are a good compromise between size and cost. A good one will set you back approximately $700.

of the music at a discrete point in time. The more samples the computer can "read" per second, the more accurate the reproduction. The higher the number of bits per sample, the better. When digitized sound is played back, the samples are converted back into sound waves you can hear. They're not exactly the same as the original wave forms, but if the sample rate and resolution is high enough, the human ear won't be able to tell the difference.

Monitor Shopping List

➤ VESA compliant for compatability

➤ Dot pitch of .28 less for image sharpness

➤ MPR II for low radiation

➤ EPA green for low power

➤ Controls on front for convenience

20. **The sales person says I should spend a little more for a graphics accelerator. What's he talking about? And if I do need one, what should I be looking for?**

—All at Sea in Atlanta

The bad news is, you probably do need one. If you're like millions of today's home PC buyers, the graphics you regularly need to run on your computer are too slow to bear without a graphics accelerator. The good news is, most new PCs already have them. And if yours doesn't, you can get one pretty cheap.

But let's backtrack a minute. You know that every PC needs graphics circuitry, right? Well, typically that graphics circuitry is SuperVGA circuitry. Most computers have it, and until the Windows interface became so popular it seemed like enough. But programs for Windows—because of the number of pixels, or "dots" they're throwing onscreen—run far slower than the character-based, plain DOS programs that came before.

Soon a whole cottage industry grew up around graphics accelerators you can buy to speed up Windows. These are just new video cards you buy to improve the SuperVGA situation you've got in your computer. Priced at under $400, think of these as a sort of "super" SuperVGA card. They'll still run all your old programs, but they also include additional chips designed specifically for speeding up Windows applications and serious drafting software like AutoCad.

These days, many computers ship with either graphics-accelerator VGA circuitry standard or as an option. If you're going to be running Windows or OS/2—and they're so popular, chances are you will be—you want it.

Video acceleration that works with your PC's "local bus" connectors, if you have them, are even more efficient. More and more new PCs are shipping with specially designed high-performance local bus slots that you can plug graphics cards, hard-disk controls, and network adapters into.

21. At the computer store they really tried to push a surge protector on me. I don't have one for my other electronic applicances; why should I buy one for the computer?

—*Cautious in Catalina*

Why should you buy a surge protector? Because you just spent $2,000 for a computer that could be destroyed by 20¢ worth of electricity, ya knucklehead!

To be kind, though, a surge protector should be bundled with every computer purchase. At $50 to $100, it's the cheapest insurance you can get. In fact, most surge protectors will actually insure you against losses caused by power surges, often for as much as $10,000.

You see, computer circuitry is very sensitive to sudden increases in voltage, much more so than most of your other electrical appliances. A surge protector shuts down the power the instant a surge is detected, preventing the excess voltage from reaching your computer.

Look for a surge protectors that meets the Underwriters Laboratories 1449 standard for TVSS. It should say so on the box.

Some surge protectors also offer protection for telephone lines. Consider buying one if you use a modem and live in lightning country. Stray voltage from a lightning bolt often travels through telephone lines into your modem and from there into your computer, turning your CPU into a 486 fricasee.

Computers are very sensitive to sudden increases in voltage, much more so than your other household appliances. A surge protector keeps that excess electricity from destroying your computer.

Be careful not to confuse a surge protectors with an uninterruptible power supply, or UPS, though. When your surge supressor trips, it shuts your system down completely, and you'll lose whatever work you haven't saved to the hard disk. If that bothers you, consider spending a few hundred dollars more for a UPS. The battery in the UPS will use its small reserve of power to give you enough time to save your work when the power dies. Most UPS systems also offer protection against power surges as well as brownouts.

22. I love my new home computer, but guess what? I forgot to buy a printer for it! I want to be able to print out letters and work reports without having to put them on a disk and carry them to the office. Can you recommend something cheap?

—Pining for Prints in Peoria

Well, the cheapest printer you can buy is a dot-matrix printer. Now we know you know what a dot matrix printer is. They've been around offices for years—loud, noisy, rhythmically whirring beasts printing line after line on miles and miles of holey tractor-feed paper. Of course, junior versions of this beast are also available for home use—and they're dirt cheap these days at well under $200—but we can't recommend anything this jarring. Even the little ones are loud. Plus, it's great to be able to print on real paper you wouldn't be embarrassed to send to Aunt Martha. (And don't you think you'll feel pretty goofy always having to strip off the holey sides from all your documents. Did you know that's called *bursting* and *decollating?* Figures.)

> *If you've got kids, consider getting an ink-jet-style printer capable of churning out color prints. Kids love printing their cool artwork.*

So that means your decision is down to ink-jet–style printers or the more sophisticated laser printers. Lasers—starting at around $500—are a hundred bucks more expensive. But if you print a lot, they do save you some money in the long run. The cost per page, which is how you measure these things, is only about a cent and a half for laser printers. Ink-jet printers, though cheaper to purchase, cost more to use, about 5 cents per page. So if you're going to be printing lots of documents, reports, letters, charts and the like, a personal laser-jet printer makes sense.

Still, if you've got kids, you may want to get a printer capable of churning out color prints. Kids love creating and passing around the amazing artistic creations they can make using kids art software. Here, color ink-jets are the choice. They're the most affordable—in fact, they're cheaper than color laser jets by thousands of dollars. Your call, though.

Printer pickins

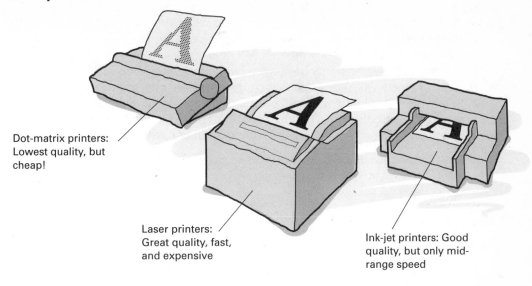

Dot-matrix printers: Lowest quality, but cheap!

Laser printers: Great quality, fast, and expensive

Ink-jet printers: Good quality, but only mid-range speed

23. **We use a tape backup system at work. Does it make sense to have one at home, too?**

—Backing up in Buffalo

It does if you're smart. Take it from the experts. During the course of writing this book in fact, one of us—and no, we're not naming names—lost two whole chapters due to sheer stupidity. This particular author didn't back up, and then the system failed. Boy, did that lead to trouble. Let's change the subject.

But the moral to the story is, don't wait for a disaster—a power surge, nasty bump, or hardware glitch—to convince you to start taking care of your data. Start doing it now because if you haven't lost any data yet, it isn't too late. If you care at all about the records you keep and all the data you store in your computer, you should care enough to back it up regularly using a reliable tape backup drive.

If you're buying a computer, pick one that has a tape drive preinstalled, even if it means sacrificing dual floppy drives. If you already own a computer, take the system back to the store and ask them to put in a tape drive for you. Or install it yourself.

Depending on whether you're buying a PC or a Mac, your tape choices vary. Macintosh users don't have much choice. For some reason, tape backup never really took hold in the Mac world. Most Mac users still use floppy disks, or back up onto a removable hard-disk drive.

On PCs, you want to make sure that the tape drive is QIC-compatible—that means it'll work with the majority of QIC-type cartridge tapes on the market. You'll also need backup software that will help you easily and painlessly copy your data to the tapes. Many backup software packages come with a feature that'll let you automatically back up your whole hard disk or just recently changed files. In other words, you set the timer and it will do it while you're at lunch. With technology this painless, you can't afford not to back up your data. Remember, it isn't what you'll do "if" that system or hard disk fails, it's "when."

Q/A

CHAPTER 2:
Hardware Hints

Hardware is the stuff made out of metal, glass, and plastic. The stuff that strains your back when you try to lift it, and drains your brain when you try to get it working. Here we cover the ins and outs of getting your new PC or Mac up and running.

24. I called tech support when I couldn't get my sound card to work and they said they can't help me because I've got an interrupt conflict. What the heck is an interrupt, how do they conflict, and how can I get them to stop?

—Desperate in Duluth

"Interrupt conflict" is a term wise techies use when they want all conversation to stop. It works like a charm. We find it extraordinarily useful for clearing cocktail parties.

Unfortunately, interrupt conflicts are also an all-too-frequent fact of life with IBM-compatibles. In fact, they've got millions of people tearing their hair out at this very minute. No wonder it's so hard to get through on those tech support lines. (Those of you using Macintosh computers may now be excused. This is just for those poor souls using PCs.)

But before we can talk about interrupt conflicts, we'd better explain (quickly!) what interrupts are and why your computer needs them. Ever wonder how the computer's microprocessor knows you're pressing a key on the keyboard when it's already doing something else? Well, the keyboard interrupts the microprocessor and sends it a signal that it needs attention. That signal has a specific frequency, which is that peripheral's (in this case, the keyboard's) interrupt setting. This is also known as an IRQ channel. And every component that may someday need the computer's attention—that includes the keyboard, the network, the CD-ROM, the sound card, the modem, and so on—needs its own IRQ channel.

> *"Interrupt conflict" is a term wise techies use when they want all conversation to stop. It works like a charm. We find it extraordinarily useful for clearing cocktail parties.*

Still don't get it? Then try to picture your CPU as the hub of a giant shipping operation. Information is brought in, processed, and shipped in and out of a variety of outside sources: the disk drive, modem, CD-ROM drive, sound card, mouse, keyboard, and the like. Each one needs its own frequency for communicating with the CPU. It's as if each peripheral had its own telephone line direct to the CPU. When the peripheral has some information to communicate, it calls the CPU. The CPU interrupts what it's doing, picks up the phone, receives the data, then continues on. That "phone line" peripherals use to signal the CPU is the interrupt channel. The call is called an interrupt request—IRQ for short.

Congratulations. Now you know as much about IRQs as some engineers. What you really need to know is that modern PCs have 16 built-in IRQs, numbered 0

Q/A

through 15. Each peripheral is assigned one of these lines. The keyboard is typically IRQ 1, your floppy disk is IRQ 6, your printer IRQ 7, and so on. When you add a peripheral like a sound card to your system, you will be asked to assign it an IRQ so that it can communicate with the CPU. Sometimes you set the IRQ by changing a switch on the circuit board before you install it. Sometimes you can set IRQs using software provided by the manufacturer.

Now what happens if you accidentally give your sound card the same IRQ as your mouse? Well, nothing, as long as they don't try to work at the same time. But as soon as they do you'll have an interrupt conflict, which means that one or the other of the devices will stop working. Maybe both. The only solution to the interrupt conflict is to find a unique interrupt for each device using the installation software it came with. That's not always possible, since you have a limited number of IRQs available, but generally with a little juggling you can do it.

If you want to save wear and tear on your hair, though, you'll let a technician install new peripheral devices for you. There's a reason why most service technicians have prematurely graying hair. Better them than you.

25. I was just in the store pricing video cards for my PC. Some cost $50, some cost $500. Are the $500 cards really ten times better? What's the difference?

—Video-free in Vermont

All computers need special electronics to create the images, graphics, text, and other pictures you see on your monitor. Some computers come with this circuitry built in. Others require an add-in circuit board, called a video card. Many computer buyers end up upgrading the quality of their displays by upgrading their video cards. In any case, video shoppers are faced with a bewildering array of choices.

Video cards differ in three main ways: resolution, color depth, and speed. All three make a world of difference in terms of the quality of images you can view with your computer, not to mention the time it takes to create them. Let's explain.

Resolution is the number of dots that can be displayed on the screen at a time. Every picture you see is made of a certain number of dots. Though it is independent of the screen size, the more dots your graphics can display at a time, the sharper your images will look. In the IBM world, the standard VGA adapter can display pictures at a resolution of 640 dots by 480 dots. A super-VGA adapter—which many PCs have built-in—increases the resolution to 800 by 600. And many high-end cards can display pictures at 1,024 by 768 and even 1,280 by 1,024 and higher.

Of course, when the number of dots on the screen goes up, the size of each dot has to go down. Pretty soon the dots become so small that the screen becomes unreadable. Also, the more dots you're trying to show at a time, the longer it takes for the circuitry to "draw" the image on your monitor. It's a matter of personal preference, but we wouldn't try to use a resolution higher than 640 by 480 on a

14-inch monitor. At 17 inches, 800 by 600 is good. And with a 20-inch monitor, 1,024 by 768 works well. The point is that if you have a 14-inch monitor, you really don't need to spend more for a card that can handle a screen resolution of 1,024 by 768—you'll never use it.

An image at different resolutions

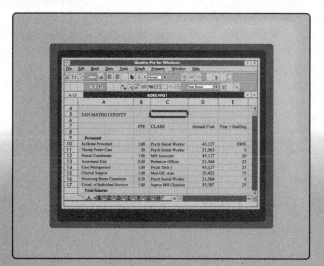

A spreadsheet in 640 × 480 resolution

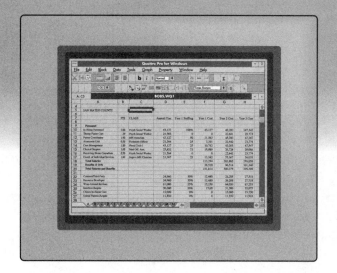

The same spreadsheet in 800 × 600 resolution

The second way video cards vary is in the number of colors they can display. Every screen is painted from a palette of available colors. Even inexpensive video cards offer palettes of at least 256 colors, all shades and combinations of red, green, and blue. And most software won't even display more than that, anyhow. If you do a lot of graphics work—photo editing or that sort of thing—you may want more colors to choose from. Fancier graphics cards offer 65,000 and even 16 million color palettes. A card that offers 16 million colors to choose from is sometimes called a true-color card because it has enough colors to render photographic images accurately. In fact, the human eye can't even see 16 million colors.

Finally, video cards differ in the time it takes to update the screen. A fast video card speeds up your computer: It's faster because your computer doesn't have to spend so much of its time drawing the screen. Speeding up screen-drawing is the whole purpose of so-called "video-accelerator" video cards on the market, by the way. They come with special chips that are designed to speed up the kinds of graphical displays used by the Windows, OS/2, and Macintosh operating systems, as well as line-drawing-intensive applications like Autodesk. You generally don't see speed increases if you use a text-based operating system like DOS. But if you use a graphical operating system, you should definitely consider an accelerated card.

You can trust the manufacturer's design specifications with regard to the screen resolution and number of colors a video card supports, but speed claims belong in the same category as fishing stories. It's better to trust an objective third party. *PC Magazine* and *MacUser* are just two magazines that perform independent benchmark tests on video cards and publish the results regularly. We advise you to check a recent issue before you buy.

It's never worth saving money by buying an off-brand video card. The circuitry may be unreliable or nonstandard. Buy a name brand card from a reputable dealer. And check recent magazine reviews to make sure the card lives up to its manufacturer's claims.

TIP

Three factors to consider when buying a video card: speed, color depth, and resolution. All contribute to the quality of the images displayed on your screen, as well as the time required for the image to appear. Don't try to save money on cheap, off-brand cards—you could end up with a substandard product and poor-quality images.

Q/A

26. **My printer jams every four or five pages. It's driving me crazy. What's wrong?**

—In a Jam in Jericho

Probably your paper. Laser printers use heating elements to dry the toner after it's applied to the page. The heat will curl cheap paper, causing it to jam the machine. Buy 20-pound bond paper that's specifically intended for copy machines or laser printers. It's more expensive than cheaper typewriter-quality paper, but you'll save yourself an infinite amount of hassle in the long run sweating over paper jams. And when you do insert the paper, make sure to do it right side up. On most high-quality paper intended for laser printers, there will be an indication of which side to print first.

Finally, if you still get frequent jams, check your paper path to make sure it's clear and clean. Sometimes labels can gum up the works. Sometimes wear and tear on the rollers and feed mechanism can cause the printer to jam all the time. In that case, you'll want to take your printer to the shop to have those parts looked at, cleaned, and possibly replaced.

Modern memory comes on little circuit boards called SIMMs, short for Single Inline Memory Modules. But you don't even have to know that to install one.

27. **I just bought a new computer. At the store they told me that I'd be able to use the old memory chips in my new system, but I've tried and they don't fit!**

—Annoyed in Albuquerque

Computer memory, or RAM, comes on microchips in various forms. Older computers used DIPs—dual inline packages. You used to have to insert these chips into the main circuit board one at a time. If you're adding DIP-style memory—and it sounds like you are—make sure you add chips of the same capacity and speed as the originals. If there's a mismatch, your computer won't work.

Modern memory comes on little circuit boards called SIMMs, single inline memory modules. Each SIMM module comes with several DIP chips glued onto it. SIMMs are easy to install. The connector slides in at a slight angle, then tilts up to lock in place. SIMMs are easy to remove, too. You don't need any special tools to do it, which makes it a snap—literally—to move SIMMs from your old machine to the new machine.

Q/A

DIPs and SIMMs

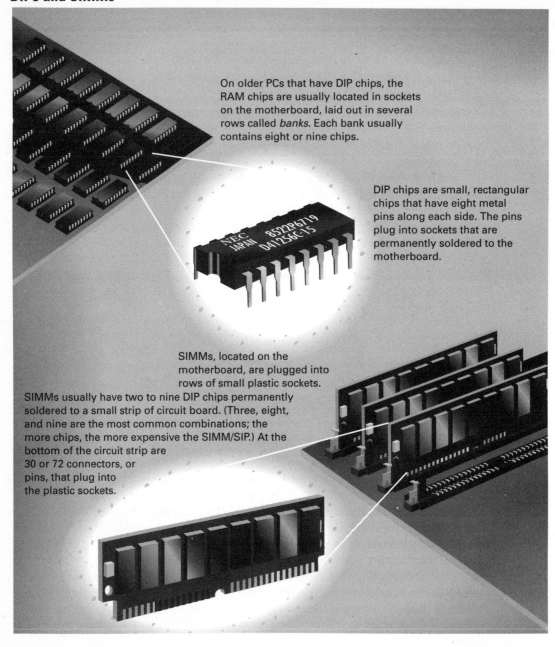

On older PCs that have DIP chips, the RAM chips are usually located in sockets on the motherboard, laid out in several rows called *banks*. Each bank usually contains eight or nine chips.

DIP chips are small, rectangular chips that have eight metal pins along each side. The pins plug into sockets that are permanently soldered to the motherboard.

SIMMs, located on the motherboard, are plugged into rows of small plastic sockets.

SIMMs usually have two to nine DIP chips permanently soldered to a small strip of circuit board. (Three, eight, and nine are the most common combinations; the more chips, the more expensive the SIMM/SIP.) At the bottom of the circuit strip are 30 or 72 connectors, or pins, that plug into the plastic sockets.

SIMMs come in 1-, 4-, 8-, 16-, and 32MB sizes. And, just like the old style memory chips, they're rated by speed. Your new computer may have certain restrictions about how you can combine SIMMs, and what speeds you can use. Always check the documentation first.

There are two different kinds of SIMMs in common usage, those with 30-pin connectors and those with 72-pin connectors. They are not interchangeable, but there are companies that will convert one style to the other for a small charge. Autotime in Portland, Oregon (503-452-8495), for example, charges $13.50 to convert a 1MB 30-pin SIMM to a 72-pin SIMM. If you're stuck with the old DIP style chips, you can get them mounted onto SIMMs, too.

28. **I finally bought a new computer. Before I sold my old machine I backed up the hard disk. But now my new machine can't read my old floppies I used to back up. Help!**

—Stranded in Scranton

Boy, isn't it confounding! Just when you've got a whole shoebox full of old floppy disks, you get a new computer that doesn't seem to work with any of them. This is true for many people buying their second PC, and especially for people going from PC to Mac and vice versa.

> *Even if disks are of the same type, data might be recorded on them differently.*

There are two different possible incompatibilities when moving data from one computer to another. The disks themselves can be incompatible, and even if the disks are the same type, the data may be recorded on them differently.

Floppy disks come in three different sizes: 8-inch, 5.25-inch, and the not particularly floppy floppy—the 3.5-inch disk. Obviously a 3.5-inch disk drive can't read an 8-inch floppy, even if you fold it in half. Don't laugh, we've known people to try it! But there are other ways to get your old data into your new computer.

There is also the matter of formatting densities, as if all this weren't annoying enough. The oldest PCs around use disks formatted in a low-capacity, double-density (DD) arrangement. Newer ones use high density (HD) disks. The two kinds of disks are incompatible, and this sounds like your problem. Look in the phone book for a "data service bureau" that can move your data from DD to HD disks, or find a friend who's willing to do it.

29. I keep my computer's main unit on the floor. Unfortunately, that's also where my dog keeps his bed. I can't move the computer for space reasons, and my wife won't let me move the dog's bed. So tell me, how do I get the dog hair out of my disk drive?

—Hirsute in Hannibal

We thank Hirsute for the question—and no, we did not make it up. We didn't make up any of these questions. These are things people really want to know. And to show our gratitude to poor Hirsute, we'll hide his true identity to our dying day.

Always remember that your computer's three greatest enemies are dirt, moisture, and heat. (We guess you could add puppy dogs and three-year-old children to the list—we've got one apiece.) But what it all really comes down to is keeping your computer clean, dry, and cool.

> *You might consider dog-proofing your PC by taping some pantyhose material in front of the vents. It won't block the free flow of air, which is critical for keeping the inside of a PC cool and hair-free.*

This question and the next two cover the details of just how to protect your computer from these three demons. So for now, let's start with Enemy No. 1: dirt, or, in this case, dog hair.

First of all, it's best to keep dirt out in the first place. Most computers have fans that draw air through the system to keep it cool. Along with the air, they also end up drawing dust, grit, and other contaminants. (Dog and cat hair have the nasty habit of melting into a sticky residue that coats the chips and circuitry inside.) You can't prevent the gradual silting up of your system, but you can slow it down. Place your computer somewhere away from all that grime. The floor is usually not the ideal spot for the PC. If you want to put it under your desk, raise it up a foot or two from the floor.

If you're still getting dog hair in the guts of it, you might consider dog proofing the PC by wrapping it in pantyhose material. It looks stupid, but it works. The fine mesh of the hose will act as a screen against dust, dog hair, and fuzzballs, without blocking the free flow of air, which is critical for keeping the PC cool. And this solution is cheap and easy. Just grab some hosiery and slip it on.

No matter what you do, though, you'll still have to clean your PC once in a while. Dust will build up on the circuit boards, acting like a blanket that can cause the components to overheat. Every year or so you should open up your computer case and vacuum up all that dust. Computer stores sell small vacuums for just that purpose.

It's easy to open the case. Nothing to be afraid of. Your manuals should explain how. Make sure to turn the computer off first. And to be extra safe, unplug it, too. When you're vacuuming, try not to knock any of the circuit boards or connectors. If you do, make sure they're properly reconnected before you close up your computer.

You won't be able to get inside certain parts of the computer, and you shouldn't. Your power supply is sealed and has a big sign on it saying something in Chinese. We don't read Chinese, but we imagine it says something like, "Whoa, stay out of here. You could really get zapped!" It's true. Stay out of there. Same thing goes for your monitor. If you can see a lot of dust inside, take it to a store where a technician who is paid to risk his life can clean it. Your hard-disk drives are sealed to keep dust and contaminants out—you can't get in to clean them, and you don't need to, anyway.

On the other hand, keyboards and mice like to be cleaned frequently. That is, you'd better like to clean them frequently or you can mess them up permanently.

Battling dirt and dust

When dust builds up on chips and circuits, it acts as a blanket, holding in the heat that the components generate. Dust and dirt can also contain chemical contaminants that conduct electricity. They may be microscopic to our eye, but they are rivers of electricity on computer circuits. They can cause an electrical short or change the logic of a circuit by creating a signal where there should be none.

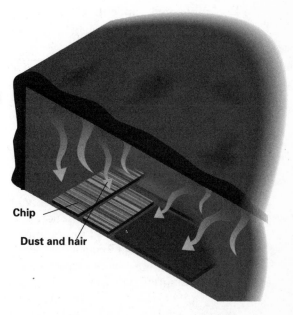

Chip

Dust and hair

Q/A

Luckily, cleaning your keyboard is simple. Check the manual to find out how to remove the keycaps. On most keyboards you can pry them off by gently pulling straight up.

It's very important that you keep track of where the keys go so you can put them back. This is key (no pun intended). Nothing is more frustrating than pressing the backspace key and getting a carriage return. Once you've removed the keycaps, it's easy to clean out the switches underneath by blasting them with compressed air. You'll find spray cans of compressed air at any photography supply store. Mice accumulate gunk inside as the ball underneath rolls around on your desk. You'll know if your mouse is dirty because the on-screen pointer starts misbehaving and jumping around like a Mexican jumping bean. Cleaning a mouse involves removing the ball underneath and polishing the rollers inside the cavity with a cotton swab dipped in denatured alcohol.

Some computer stores sell computer cleaning kits. They're usually as over-priced as they are convenient. Of course, for real convenience you can have the store clean the PC for you. It may cost a bit more, but you're worth it.

TIP

Don't try to get inside the power supply of your computer, or even poke at it with a screwdriver or other metal object. Even if your computer is unplugged, capacitors inside the unit can hold an electrical charge strong enough to injure or even kill you.

---

30. **I just spilled coffee into my keyboard! I turned off the computer immediately, of course, but is it safe to turn it back on? How do I get the keyboard working again?**

—*Creamed in Colorado*

Well, was it black coffee, or did you have cream and sugar in it? Strangely enough, if you like your joe black, you can probably let your keyboard dry out and it will work fine. Cream and sugar, on the other hand, will leave a sticky residue that's a bear to clean out. If you've spilled something sticky anywhere in your computer, we strongly recommend that you let a qualified service technician do the cleaning.

When it comes to liquids, your computer is just like any electrical appliance—the combination will produce shocking results. If you spill anything into the main unit of your computer, turn it off pronto. Mop up any obvious puddles, then bring it in for service. This is not a mess you want to clean up by yourself.

31. When I put my hand on the side of the computer it seems really warm. Is this something I should worry about? Do computers ever catch fire?

—Pittsburgh Pyrotechnical

Look on the bright side. Now you can cook breakfast on your machine while you wait for your spreadsheet to recalculate. How's that for high-tech efficiency?

Of course, it's okay for a computer to be warm to the touch. There's a lot of electronics working in there, and electronics generate heat. But your computer shouldn't feel hot. For one thing, heat accelerates your computer's aging process, and a well-designed computer case should dissipate heat well enough to keep the PC from getting hot. If it is hot, that's a sign of trouble brewing.

Pop open the computer and check the fans. When the computer's on, they should be turning. Almost all computers have at least one fan inside or near the power supply. (If you can't see the fan, you can always hear it!) Your computer may also have a second fan near the microprocessor. If a fan dies, your computer can get as hot as a sauna, which will inevitably cause some of the electronics inside to fry and fail. The first symptom is often a case that is unusally hot to the touch.

Even if a fan is working, the air intake grate on your computer could be blocked. It needs at least three inches of clearance all around it. These grates are usually located on the back of the computer. Some tower cases (those are the cases that stand tall) have intakes in front, disguised by a plastic grill.

Some of the newer CPUs run pretty hot, too, particularly fast 486 and Pentium CPUs. When you jam millions of transistors on a chip that's a half an inch square you're bound to generate some heat. As long as you buy a well-designed case with plenty of room for air to travel around inside, you shouldn't have anything to worry about.

Keeping your computer cool

Ever wonder what makes that whirring noise when your computer is turned on? It's the power supply—or, more specifically, the fan inside the power supply that keeps the PC's "engine" from overheating.

Fan

There's an easy way to tell if your microprocessor is running hot. Run your computer for an hour or two, then turn it off, open the case, and touch the chip. If you're worried it will burn off your fingerprints, it's too hot to run. In that case, buy an inexpensive fan that attaches directly to the chip and will keep it within specifications. If you can't touch the chip because it has fins on top, that's good. Those fins are part of a heat sink, a little contraption intended to carry heat away from the chip. This is a sign that your PC is well built. If you've got one, rejoice in your good fortune.

> *When you jam millions of transistors on a chip that's a half an inch square, you're bound to generate some heat.*

Laptop computers operate at a higher temperature than desktops. They don't contain fans, and the cramped quarters don't dissipate heat as well. For this reason, laptops usually include expensive "low-power" chips, which is just one more reason why little laptops cost so much more than desktops. Laptops can, however, still feel warm to the touch, usually on the underside that comes into close contact with the main circuit board.

If your laptop suddenly seems to be getting hotter and hotter that could mean that the battery is short circuited. Pop it out if you can and make sure that the contacts aren't accidentally connected to each other. If the condition persists contact your dermatologist, or better yet, your service technician.

32. Every time my husband vacuums, the computer monitor starts to act weird. What's going on?

—Vacuous in Vacaville

The motors in your vacuum cleaner are probably generating electrical interference with your monitor, perhaps through your home's electrical wiring. You probably don't have to worry about the interference damaging either your monitor or computer. It's just annoying.

We suggest you might try to get your husband to plug the vac into another outlet farther from where you're working. You can also buy a power conditioner, which will filter out interference. Or you can just turn off the computer, sit back, sip a lemonade, and watch your husband work. It certainly beats trying to balance the checkbook, and it can be just as much fun as polishing off demons in Doom.

33. I usually leave my screen on all day. Do I need a screen saver to protect it? What exactly is it saving my screen from?

—Blank in Biloxi

In the dark old days of computing (before 1988), computer screens had a tendency to "burn-in." If you left an image of, say, a word processing document on them for an extended period of time, the screen's phosphors would begin to retain the image. Then you'd end up with a monitor that permanently displays that ghostly image of the document, even if it's shut off. Screen savers were invented about this time to prevent burn-in.

Screen savers are small programs that run behind the scenes, waiting for you to stop typing or clicking around on the computer. After a period of inactivity you specify, the screen saver kicks in and blanks the screen to prevent burn-in. These quickly became popular for security reasons, too. Having the screen blank out after a few seconds or so was a great way to keep nosey coworkers from glancing over your shoulder at your confidential memos.

Computer programmers, never content to leave well enough alone, began to embellish these early screen savers. Instead of just blanking the screen, these enhanced savers filled the empty screen with entertaining animations. As long as the animations didn't stay in the same place for very long there'd be no danger of their images getting burned into the phosphors.

Many computer users are hooked on their screensavers—not because they're necessary—they're not—but because they're fun.

As computer monitors have evolved, the danger of images burning into them has diminished. Your VGA monitor is unlikely to ever burn in. But computer users have gotten hooked on their screen savers. Not because they're necessary—they're not—but because they're fun.

Today you can choose from screen savers that put flying toasters, cartoon characters, even movies on your screen whenever you take a break. It's just one more way to make your PC more fun.

But if you're using your screensaver all night, as well as all day, you need to rethink this. Leaving your computer on all night while you sleep is just a huge waste of power. Anticipating this, many of the newer "green" monitors on the market automatically power-down, or "sleep," after a certain amount of time.

Q/A

34. I've heard about accuracy problems with certain computer chips. Can I trust my computer with my checkbook?

—Off Balance in Orono

In late 1994, word of a mathematical problem in Intel's top-of-the-line Pentium CPU swept the computer world like wildfire. Millions of people in professional and home office settings wondered whether they had wasted money on a Pentium PC that couldn't divide numbers correctly. Despite Intel's protestations that the average user would stand a greater chance of being hit by lightning than being bit by the Pentium bug, users demanded replacement chips. It was a public relations nightmare for Intel, and it shook consumer confidence in the reliability of computers.

The truth is, all computers make mistakes. All computer chips contain bugs. There's also no such thing as mistake-free software, either. We know that's bad news, but it's best you hear it now. People make computers, and people aren't perfect.

> *The truth is, all computers make mistakes. All computer chips contain bugs. There's also no such thing as mistake-free software, either.*

The good news is that most of the time your computer's errors are harmless. They rarely affect your data. And when they do, you'll know it. A subtle change in your bank balance is highly unlikely. It's much more likely that your data will disappear altogether. Or your bank balance will become $10,000,000. (Gee, how come the bank's computers never make mistakes like this?)

In other words, don't worry.

35. I spend a lot of time at the keyboard. Am I going to get that nasty carpal tunnel syndrome?

—Cramped in Catalina

Gosh, we hope not! We spend more time typing than anyone we know.

Carpal tunnel syndrome is one of several injuries caused by repetitive motions, like typing on a keyboard all the time. Repetitive stress injuries, or RSIs, are common among butchers, assembly line workers, Nintendo players, and computer users.

When it comes to computers, carpal tunnel syndrome is the most common kind of RSI. It's caused by spending too much time at the keyboard, and is exacerbated by holding your wrists at unnatural angles for too long. There's a channel that passes along the underside of your wrist called the carpal tunnel. The tunnel contains a nerve which can become irritated, leading to tingling, numbness and pain in your wrist. Mild cases of carpal tunnel syndrome are annoying. A serious case can be debilitating. Some people sue their employers and make big money because of this. But trust us, they're in too much pain to enjoy the money.

If you spend a lot of time at your computer, there are things you should do to prevent carpal tunnel syndrome and reduce physical fatigue. First, get a chair and desk that are at comfortable heights. Your feet should rest flat on the floor. Your legs should bend at a 90-degree angle—so that your thighs are neither tilted up or down. When your hands rest on the keyboard, your arms should also be bent at a 90-degree angle.

To protect against carpal tunnel syndrome, buy a wrist rest for your keyboard that elevates your wrists so that your hands are neither tilted up nor down. If you use a mouse a lot, you'll also want a mouse pad that supports your wrist.

The carpal tunnel

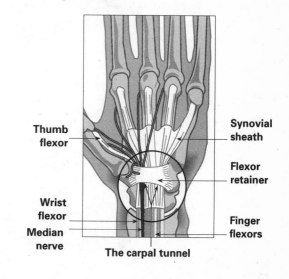

Thumb flexor

Wrist flexor

Median nerve

The carpal tunnel

Synovial sheath

Flexor retainer

Finger flexors

Your monitor should be at eye level and far enough away so that you need to stretch your arm to full length to touch it. That's about two feet.

Most importantly, take a lot of breaks. Every hour get up from the computer and stretch. Take a walk, get some fresh air. Blink your eyes. Did you know that people blink less when they stare at computer monitors? That's one of the reasons your eyes get tired. Also, spend some time looking out into the distance. Focusing at the same distance for hours at a time is very fatiguing. Your eyes relax when they're focused at a faraway object.

Finally, if you do start feeling some twinges in your wrists, consult your doctor immediately. He or she can prescribe a wrist brace that will keep things from getting worse.

Computers can be so compelling that it's easy to lose track of time. We often find ourselves sitting down for a minute or two and looking up hours later. Don't let your enthusiasm for this new machine cause problems that could keep you from using it. Make sure you've got a safe and comfortable work area and take lots of breaks. Your wrists (and spouse) will thank you.

The zero-injury home-computer setup

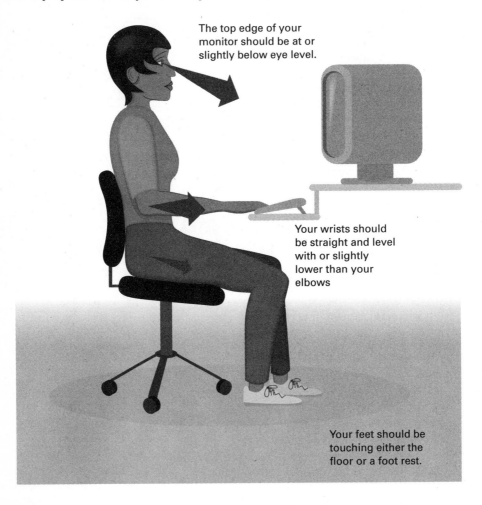

The top edge of your monitor should be at or slightly below eye level.

Your wrists should be straight and level with or slightly lower than your elbows

Your feet should be touching either the floor or a foot rest.

36. Someone told me that I should keep my computer monitor at arm's length. Literally. Should I be worried? Is my computer really going give me cancer?

—Nearsighted in Nevada

This is scary stuff. There's some research to show that the extremely low frequency electrical waves emitted by computer monitors (and electric blankets, clock radios, high-tension wires, and a million other things) might be harmful to humans. Some studies even suggest they can cause leukemia and miscarriages. The jury's still out, but why take a chance, especially if you're pregnant?

If you're buying a new monitor, look for one that conforms to the tough Swedish MPR II standards for emissions. But if you already own a monitor that doesn't conform, forget about buying an expensive screen for the front of it that's supposed to reduce radiation. Most of the worrisome stuff comes from the back of the monitor, so it won't help much.

There's some research to show that the extremely low-frequency electrical waves emitted by computer monitors (and electric blankets, clock radios, high-tension wires, and a million other things) might be harmful to humans.

The good news is that when you double your distance from the source, you receive a lot less radiation. Stay a couple of feet away from your monitor and even the most pessimistic doomsayers believe you're safe.

If you're really worried, you can buy an inexpensive radiation monitor and take your own measurements. Aware Electronics Corp. (302-655-3800) makes one with a Windows interface for around $150. You could even start a business checking your friends' computers.

37. I turn my computer off when I'm not using it, but a neighbor told me it's better to leave it on all the time because it won't wear out as fast. Is that true?

—Doubting in Destin

Somewhere somebody got the idea that it's better for your to leave your computer on all the time. This canard just keeps resurfacing. So let's blow this "fowl" rumor out of the water once and for all.

The "leave it on" theory is based on the observation that light bulbs always seem to burn out just when you turn them on. Turning electronics on, the theory goes, is stressful. So never turn them off and they're less likely to fail. What hooey.

First of all, your computer is not a light bulb. The electronics inside are not going to burn out in our lifetime. The truth is that computers become obsolete long before they wear out. There are some things that do suffer wear from starting and stopping. The bearings in your hard drive, for instance, expand and contract as they heat up and cool down, and that will wear them out eventually. You could probably increase their longevity by leaving the drive running all the time. But adding a year or two of life to a hard drive that's going to last for decades isn't really necessary.

And there's a far greater price to be paid by leaving your computer on all the time. Just check your electric bill. A computer can draw 100 to 200 watts while it's on. A laser printer takes ten times that. Leaving them on all the time is a big waste of energy and money. And since it doesn't add appreciably to the longevity of the machine, why do it? If you're not going to use a computer for more than a few hours, turn it off already!

> *First of all, your computer is not a lightbulb. The elctronics inside are not going to burn out in our lifetime. The truth is that computers become obsolete long before they wear out.*

Computers use a lot of power in this country. Multiply 100 watts times 50 million computers and you can see the magnitude of the problem. The Environmental Protection Agency has been effective in convincing manufacturers to build computers that use less power, and reduce their power consumption when they're not being used. These Green PCs go a long way to cutting electric bills. Look for the Green PC decal when you buy your next computer or printer.

38. **Now what do I do? The computer says to press any key to continue. Am I missing something? Where's the ANY key?**

—*Gump in Gilroy*

We had to throw this question in. We doubt that anyone's ever asked it seriously, but it keeps cropping up whenever magazines write stories about silly tech support questions.

Just in case Forrest Gump really is reading this book, let's go on record stating that there is no "ANY" key. When your computer asks you to press any key, they mean press the key of your choice. Any key will do.

39. I bought a Macintosh because the dealer said it would be easy to add hard-disk capacity. Well, I've run out of room on my original drive. Now how do I add another?

—Willing in Wheeling

It is easy. Apple had the great foresight to build in an external SCSI port on every Macintosh since the Mac Plus shipped in 1985. So you know, SCSI stands for small computer systems interface and is pronounced *scuzzy*. This is the most unfortunate acronym in the whole history of computing. For a while Apple tried to convince everyone to pronounce it *sexy*, but the name never took hold.

SCSI is a marvelous thing. A single SCSI connector on the back of your machine can support up to seven devices, each attached to the other like a daisy chain.

The seven can be made up of any combination of peripherals, as long as they all have a SCSI interface built in. That means you can add three hard-disk drives, a scanner, a CD-ROM, and a plotter to your machine—all without breaking a sweat.

Adding a hard drive to a Macintosh is as easy as plugging it in to the back of the machine. There are a couple of things to keep in mind. Because the SCSI chain can vary in length, the beginning and end of the chain has to be plugged-up—or terminated—by plugging in a little resistor. The beginning of the chain is the computer itself, and is almost always properly terminated. It's up to you to terminate the other end of the chain. Get your dealer to show you how.

Also, in order for the computer to talk to the various SCSI devices on the chain, each device has to have a unique identification number, or ID. SCSI IDs range from 0 to 7. The computer (or SCSI card in the case of a PC) is always 0. Most SCSI devices have some way to change IDs in case of a conflict.

When you add external SCSI devices to a Mac, it's important to always turn them on before you turn on the computer. That way the Mac will recognize them when it comes on.

You can add a SCSI interface to your IBM-PC compatible, too, but as always, adding capabilities to the PC may require some trial and error and troubleshooting. The SCSI card will have to be configured to work with your unique system setup. And since the PC operating system doesn't come with built-in SCSI support, you will have to add software to tell it how to access the SCSI devices. Every SCSI card and device for the PC comes with its own software.

SCSI and the Macintosh go together like love and marriage, maybe even better. SCSI on the PC could be grounds for a divorce. If you want to use a SCSI interface with a PC, you'd be best off buying it as part of a whole new system. On a PC, installing SCSI devices and keeping them working can be really tough.

40. **My computer sounds like a 747 taking off. It whines and whinnies and rattles and buzzes. I ended up buying long keyboard and monitor cables and keeping the computer in the closet. Is there anything I can do to keep the noise down?**

—Hard of Hearing in Hollywood

This is the kind of question we try to get our callers to act out on the radio show. Nothing livens up a computer program more than a caller making funny noises. It doesn't help us diagnose the problem much, but it sure is entertaining.

It's not unusual for people to take their first computer home and react with horror when they turn it on. That machine that sounded so quiet in the store sounds like a Mack truck in the living room. It's not that the machine's any noisier, it's just quieter at home.

Your computer's fan should make a steady whirring sound. If you hear any clanking or knocking, the fan's blades may be striking a wire or other protuberance. This is not good.

Computers aren't quiet. Each one makes different noises, but it helps to know which noises are normal and which are a sign of trouble. Here's a list of the noisemaking items in your computer, and our best print approximation of how they should sound.

One of the noisemakers in your computer is the fan. It's a necessary evil—without the fan your computer would overheat. We've known very noise-sensitive people to replace the fan in their computers with quieter models, but that's hardly worth the effort. Of course, some computer makers skip the fan to make their computers quieter, but we don't recommend buying one of them. You don't want to court overheating problems.

The only computers we know of that don't need fans are laptops. Most laptops are quieter, but see question 5 before you replace your desktop PC with a portable.

Your fan should make a steady whirring sound. If you hear any clanking or knocking, the fan's blades may be striking a wire or other protuberance. This is not good. Open the case and correct the matter. Occasionally the bearings in a fan will wear and it will begin to rumble. That's the time to replace the fan. If it stops working, so will your computer.

The other big noisemaker in a computer is the hard drive. It seems like every hard disk makes a different noise, and almost all of them sound annoying. Hard drives tend to whine. Sometimes they even vibrate. Many hard drives make small clicks when you access the disk. All these sounds are normal.

When your hard drive suddenly starts to rattle, that's when you should worry. The bearings in a hard drive can wear out. Before they fail entirely they'll usually start to sound funny. That's when you should act fast to make a backup copy of your data, before the bearings freeze up entirely. But there's such a wide variation of normal sounds that you'll just have to rely on your instincts as to whether the noise signals a problem.

Floppy-disk drives make grinding sounds when accessing the disk. It's annoying but normal.

Your computer monitor should be absolutely silent. Any pops, clicks, or whines emanating from the screen are a sure sign of trouble brewing. Take it to the shop for a professional diagnosis.

In general, any abrupt change in the quality or quantity of noise coming from your computer is a trouble signal that you should attend to.

The only way to quiet a noisy computer down is to move it away from you. You don't want to wrap it in anything. That would cause overheating. And don't put it inside anything else—like a chest, say—unless there's good ventilation. Of course, if air can get in and out, so can sound. So you may have come up with the best solution of all, getting a long cord and sticking the PC in the closet.

TIP

The biggest noisemaker in your computer is the fan. It's a necessary evil—without the fan your computer would overheat. We've known very noise-sensitive people to replace the fan in their computers with quieter models, but that's hardly worth the effort.

---

41. **Every time I install a new toner cartridge in my laser printer, I have to throw away the old one. It seems like a terrible waste. Can't I just get it refilled with toner?**

—Out of Toner in Toronto

You don't want to refill toner cartridges. Toner can make a real mess. But do recycle used-up cartridges. Most companies that sell cartridges let you seal up the old cartridge and mail it back for recycling.

42. My PC is a couple of years old. It's starting to seem really slow, especially with the new software I've been buying lately. Do I have to buy a new computer, or is there an easy way to speed the old one up?

—Older in Boulder

There is no shortage of ways to speed up your computer. In fact, there's a whole cottage industry of hardware companies dying to help you. But how much are you willing to spend to do it?

If you've got an IBM-PC compatible based on a 386 or 486 chip, you may be able to actually replace the CPU with a newer, faster chip. This isn't cheap, but it is the simplest way to get a major speed increase. Cyrix Corporation (800-GO-CYRIX) makes a line of chips designed to replace out-of-date 386 microprocessors. The Cyrix upgrades range in price from $200 to $300, depending on which 386 you're upgrading. As long as your microprocessor isn't soldered into the main circuit board, it's a simple matter of pulling it out and popping in the upgrade. You can even do it yourself. Honest. We're seeing a speed increase of about 80 percent using these Cyrix upgrades. That might be enough to make you happy.

> *Don't be tempted by advertisements that claim to upgrade an old 286 PC to 386 or 486 levels. These are the digital equivalent of the ads for converting your car to use water instead of fuel. It just can't happen.*

If you have a 486-based machine, Intel offers something they call the Overdrive Processor. This chip fits into a free socket on the motherboard of your computer. It disables the old processor and takes over, doubling or tripling the speed of your old PC. If you don't have an Overdrive socket (your computer manual should tell you) you can swap out your old chip and replace it with the upgrade. Intel's Overdrive Processors range from $150 to $550 depending on speed, and they're sold over the counter in many computer stores.

Intel is also making a Pentium upgrade for 486 computers, but we don't think it is a cost-effective upgrade. Stick with the Overdrive upgrades.

If you've got a 286 you may be tempted by advertisements that claim to upgrade your PC to a 386- or 486-class machine. Don't be. These are the digital equivalent of the ads for converting your car to using water for fuel. The technical details are not worth going into. Just trust us, if you want to upgrade your 286 you'll need to replace more than just the processor.

If your computer is a 286 machine or an old Apple Lisa or Amiga or something, you're probably better off just shelling out the cash for a fast new 486 or Macintosh computer. Most of the hot new software on the shelves requires a lot of power, after all. And we're betting that some of that old PC's components—hard disk, modem, monitor—are getting too ancient to run reliably anyhow.

A cheaper idea is adding more memory, which will considerably cut the time it takes your applications to do things. If you upgrade the amount of system memory (RAM) in your system from just 4MB to 8MB, you'll see a pretty dramatic improvement in speed in your Windows application programs. Also, if you don't already have one, replacing your plain old display adapter with a speedy "graphics accelerator" card can make a world of difference in Windows' performance.

Installing a memory chip

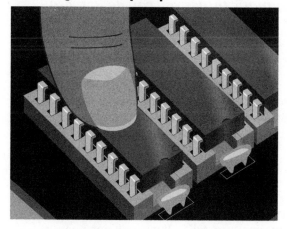

And think about replacing your hard disk, too: Add a faster one and you'll find that accessing your data takes much less time. Plus, regular use of disk repair and defragmentation software on that hard disk will make it more efficient too. Finally, a faster modem means faster downloads and, if you're lucky, cheaper phone bills.

You know, too many people just give up and get a new system when the old one they've got gets sluggish. What a waste of dough. If you bought your 386 or 486 system within the last few years, odds are you can pump it up with a little investment. (Of course, if you're going to be sinking a grand or more into your upgrades, maybe you should shell out for a new system and give yours to your local school or church. Or you could be artsy and turn it into a giant doorstop.)

43. **Windows keeps telling me I'm out of memory, but I just bought a new hard drive and I know there's lots of room left. I don't get it.**

—Stumped in Stamford

We get this one all the time. Hard-disk space is often confused with memory, probably because computer advertisements and computer magazines for novices wrongly assume everyone knows the difference.

So let's clear it up once and for all. Memory usually refers to the bunch of chips inside your computer known as RAM. RAM is very fast, but expensive, about $35 per megabyte. All the instructions and data your microprocessor is working on are stored in RAM for quick access. But because everything in RAM disappears when you turn the power off, you also need long-term storage. That's where your disk drives come in. Programs and data are stored on disk when they're not being used by your CPU. Disk storage is slow, but relatively cheap, under $1 per megabyte, so you can afford to have lots. We recommend 8MB of RAM, 340MB of hard-disk storage.

Now. If you're getting out-of-memory error messages, that means your RAM is full. If you run out of disk space, you'll get a completely different message, something like "Out of Disk Space."

> *Upgrading an older 33 MHz 486 CPU to run at double the speed is one of the most dramatic things you can do to speed up your computer.*

When you get an out-of-memory error message there are several things you can do. First, close all the windows and applications you're not using. If that doesn't free enough memory to continue, you might want to save your work and restart your computer. This will give you a fresh start and will often clear up out-of-memory conditions.

If you get out-of-memory error messages in DOS, you need a memory manager. Memory managers reorganize memory usage to make it more efficient, and can usually fix those out-of-memory blues. DOS 6.0 and later comes with MEM-MAKER. Type MEMMAKER to automatically install it. If you still don't have enough memory, you might want to buy a third-party memory manager—they do an even better job of finding more memory. We like Netroom from Helix and Quarterdeck's QEMM.

Windows users can increase the amount of available memory by using virtual memory, sometimes known as a swap disk. Check your virtual memory settings by opening the Enhanced Control Panel from within Windows. Increasing the size of the swap disk will often eliminate memory problems, but can slow down your computer. Some Macintosh models also support virtual memory. Use the Memory Control Panel to turn it on.

Virtual memory uses hard-disk storage to simulate RAM. But because the hard disk is much slower than RAM, virtual memory is much slower than the real thing. If you find yourself relying on virtual memory all the time you might want to look into buying more RAM.

Both Windows and Macintosh systems should start with 8MB. In the Windows world you'll probably never need more than 16MB of RAM. Truly maxed-out systems sometimes have as much as 32MB but that's probably overkill. Macintosh computers can use much more. We've seen graphic artists complain of only having 128MB of RAM in their Macs! But we think you'll be just fine with between 8MB and 16MB.

44. **Help! When I turn on my computer, it just sits there. Nothing happens. So now I'm afraid to turn it off and back on again. What do I do?**

—Petrified in Providence

No wonder you're scared! You paid something like a couple of grand for the thing, and then it does nothing when you turn it on? How do you sleep at night? You know, any number of things could be wrong with your computer, but the potential problems do vary in seriousness from the "not very" category to "quick! get out the checkbook." So let's try to narrow it down.

Pardon our asking, but are you sure the computer's plugged in? Sounds stupid, but thousands of people who call computer technical support every day have the same problem. Whenever you have a computer glitch—or a printer, monitor, or keyboard glitch, for that matter—make sure the danged thing's plugged in. That means that the plug is securely attached both into your wall socket and into the back of the device that you're concerned about.

If the computer still doesn't work, make sure there's not a floppy inside of the disk drive. Computers, when they start up, are looking for a particular set of instructions to tell them what to do. Usually, those instructions are in what's known as the boot sector of the hard disk. Some floppy disks are "bootable," too, but you've got to make them that way intentionally by typing **/S** after the format a: command.

No floppy? Okay. Don't get scared, but now we want you to keep a close eye on what happens with the lights on the front of your PC when you turn it on. You see, whenever you turn your computer on, the CPU checks to make sure everything is okay. It starts with the hard disk, then the floppy, then the CD-ROM if you have one, then the keyboard's NUMLOCK and CAPSLOCK keys. You can tell by the order of the little lights that go on. Most computers that fail will also let you know there's a problem by beeping a few times. Check your manual to find out what those beeps mean.

This is a handy thing to know. Say one day your computer goes on, but the lights never make it to the floppy stage. Then you know something is either wrong with your main system motherboard circuitry, or it's your hard disk. If no light comes on, there may be something wrong with the internal power supply that feeds the wattage into your computer. Not that you can do anything about these disasters, but it pays to have at least an idea of what's wrong with your computer before you let the repair people start tinkering with it. At the very least you'll save on hourly fees.

45. I know it's a little thing, but my computer's clock is always wrong. I have to set it every time I turn it on. Is there something I can do to make it more accurate?

—Time Conscious in Tecumseh

Maybe you're wondering why your computer even needs a clock in the first place. After all, you probably have a watch or clock radio within viewing distance of your PC. But PCs and Macs need to tell time, too. For example, every time you create and save a file, that file is stamped with the current time and date. That's helpful when you want to find the latest version of a document. Computers also use the clock to schedule backups, help you manage your appointments, and a whole lot more. It's not the end of the world when your computer's clock is inaccurate, but it is the kind of minor annoyance that causes some people to go ballistic after a while.

> *If you set the time, but it keeps drifting off by more than a few minutes each week, you probably have something wrong with the little "crystal" chip in your computer that's in charge of keeping time. But replacing one of these intricate gadgets definitely isn't worth it.*

You can check and set a PC's time from DOS by typing **TIME** at the C: prompt. In Windows open the Date/Time Control Panel. On a Mac, open the Date & Time Control Panel.

If you set the time but it keeps drifting off by more than a few minutes each week, you probably have something wrong with the little "crystal" chip in your computer that's responsible for keeping up with the time. Replacing one of these intricate little gadgets really isn't worth it.

You can buy software that will automatically correct your clock. Turns out most inaccurate computer clocks lose or gain time at a predictable rate. These programs figure out what that rate is, then make an adjustment whenever you turn on the machine. Your local computer store should carry one of these programs, and there are free versions available on most online services.

46. **Whoops. While my son was away at college I tried to use his computer. I seem to have gotten a disk stuck in the disk drive and I can't get it out. Help me fix it before he gets back!**

—Stuck in Stockton

Don't you hate when that happens? But it happens to the best of us. With Macs, freeing that stuck floppy is fairly easy. There's usually a little hole near where the floppy goes in. Find it, and gently insert the tip of a bent-up paper clip or the end of safety pin or bobby pin into it. That should do the trick. Similarly, a PC disk has a little button you can press to eject the disk, just as your tape or audio CD player does.

If neither method works for PC or Mac, you may be in trouble. Don't try to force it, because you can end up knocking the drive out of alignment. That's much worse than temporarily having a disk stuck in there, trust us.

So take a deep breath and pry off the cover of the floppy drive, called the panel. Check your manual or call the company to figure out how best to do this. Then you'll be able to see a little more clearly what it is that's blocking the floppy and whether you can easily remove it. If it looks too tough—remember, don't force it—bite the bullet and take the computer to the shop. (And you should know, floppies aren't the only things that get stuck in disk drives. If you've got little kids in the house, it's possible they've stuck something little inside the drive that's messing things up. Take it in.)

47. **When I move my mouse around in Windows the arrow jerks around so much I can hardly use it. Hey, I'm getting whiplash here. What's wrong?**

—Distracted in Daytona

Cleaning a mouse

It's entirely possible you have a bad case of dirty mouse ball! Seriously. A mouse ball is a little ball bearing inside your mouse that helps it move smoothly. When its ball and the rollers behind it get dirty, they start sticking and not rolling right. This could be your problem. Happily, it's easy to clean your mouse ball. Just remove the little plate on the bottom of your mouse. The little ball should fall right out.

Now pick out all the nasty stuff that's stuck to the mouse ball and the rollers behind it. Gross, isn't it? Probably there's a lot of hair, dirt, and sticky stuff stuck to them. (Didn't we tell you not to drink cola near a computer?) Use a cotton swab and a little rubbing alcohol to get the really stubborn stuff out. Then pop the ball back in, replace the plate, and your mouse pointer should be flying around smoothly in no time.

48. **I'll confess it. I kind of like to play games on my computer. My husband gave me a joystick for Christmas to help improve my score. My computer has a joystick port, two of them, in fact, but I can't get the joystick to work in either of them.**

—*Joyless in Joliet*

Not much joy in a joystick that won't work, is there? Lucky for your addictions, the problem is a common one and easy to fix.

Disabling a game port is a tough job, but someone's got to do it.

We assume that by "joystick port" you're referring to a "game port." Many new multimedia PC owners end up with two of these game port plugs on their computers, and that's a problem. First, there's the one that came standard with the PC, and then there's usually a second one that comes on the back of the sound card. Having double the game ports, in this case, means just the opposite of having double the fun. You're going to have to actually disable one of the game ports so the games you play know which one to play with.

Disabling a game port may sound like a tough job, but someone's got to do it. If that someone's you, turn off and unplug your machine, grit your teeth and pop open your main system unit. Then, locate the sound card. It will be the one with the plugs in back that lead to speakers, mikes, and the like. Check the sound card manual for information on how to find a "jumper" on the card that will effectively turn off the gameport. A jumper is just a set of two pins that you can turn on or off by changing how a little band fits around them.

As more and more sound cards come out with software configurable features that let you change things like game port features without popping the hood of your computer, this will get easier. Until then though, just grin and bear it. (And if you own a Mac, be glad you do. Macs don't have game ports. Mac game controllers plug into the Apple Desktop Bus, just like your keyboard and mouse.)

49. What are all those funny-looking keys on my computer's keyboard supposed to be? What's their purpose? I know you guys always say a computer
is just a glorified electric typewriter, but these keys sure don't look like the
ones on my old IBM Selectric!

—Pecked-Out in Pittsburgh

Well, that'll teach you to take us too literally. With as many as 101 keys on a computer keyboard compared to the typewriter's 45, there's a lot more going on. But
it's not too complicated.

In addition to the keys you remember from beginners' typing in high school,
you'll find a set of numeric keys to the right of the standard keyboard. These keys
are called the "numeric keypad." They're just like the keys on an adding machine.
And they're there because people often spend a lot of time typing in numbers.
The keypad arrangement makes it easier.

But the really odd thing about a computer keyboard is its collection of function keys, the ones that start with the letter *F.* Those keys—ranging from F1 to
F10, or F1 to F12 in some cases—are either lined up across the top of the keyboard or along the left side. Either way, these are special keys that many applications use in various ways. Windows, as a rule, uses the F1 key for "help"—that is,
press F1 and whatever Windows application you're in will generally display a
"help" screen with hints and tips. How the other keys are used vary from program to program.

And speaking of strange new keys, there's the matter of Esc (escape), Alt
(alternate) and Ctrl (control) keys. They're used, alone or in combination with
other keys, to issue commands to the program that's currently running.

The Esc key is often used like a cancel command. You can press ESC when
you want to stop whatever's going on. It may not always work, that's up to the
software developer, but it's always worth a try.

The Alt and Ctrl keys work like the Shift key: you hold them down while you
type other keys to produce something called Alt and Ctrl key combinations. For
example, when you press the Ctrl and C keys, you're issuing a Ctrl+C command. In
DOS that's usually used to interrupt the current process. In Windows, menu items
often have Ctrl key substitutes to save you time. If you take a look at the menu,
you'll see each shortcut listed to the right of the menu command it replaces.

Actually this shortcut thing began in the Macintosh world. Besides the usual
complement of Esc, Ctrl, and Alt keys (on the Mac the Alt key is also labeled
Option) the Mac also comes with something called a Command key. It's found to
the left of the space bar, marked with an Apple icon, or something that looks like
a freeway interchange ( ). The Command key works the same way as a Control
key on a PC. Geez, we wish they could have talked this out and came up with a
single standard *before* they inflicted this stuff on us.

There are also some keys on the keyboard that probably won't work like you think they will. One is the Enter (or Return) key. Typists will recall that it's the "return" or "carriage return" key that you hit after you've finished a line of typing. But computer software moves to the next line automatically, as soon as the last one is finished. You only use Enter at the end of a paragraph. (You also use Enter to signal the computer you're finished typing in a command, as in typing WIN and then Enter to start Windows.)

Your computer keyboard may have other unusual keys. Many PC keyboards have Print Screen, Scroll Lock, Break, and Pause keys. These keys are vestiges of the bad old days of DOS, and aren't of much use in modern software.

Your keyboard may also have keys designed to help you quickly move through documents. These are the Page Up, Page Down, Home, End and Arrow keys. Exactly what these keys do varies from program to program, but generally they work like this: Page Up and Down will move the text on the screen down or up by a page. That's right. Page Down moves the text up. Page Up moves the text down. It sounds wrong, but trust us, it'll make sense when you try it. Home moves you to the beginning of a line. End moves you to the end of a line. And the arrow keys move the cursor one letter at a time in any direction.

You'll also notice Insert and Delete keys. Again, what they do depends on the software you're using. In word processors, Insert changes the way new text is added to the document. Press Insert once and every letter you type will replace a letter, that's called the "overwrite" mode. Press it again, and the letters you type will squeeze into the existing text, shifting it right, that's called the "insert" mode. Delete is a backwards backspace. Instead of deleting the character to the left of the cursor, it deletes the character to the right. All this may sound confusing while you're reading it, but it all makes much more sense when you try it.

Your new keyboard may sport other specialized keys. Check your manual for more information.

50. **I didn't buy a mouse with my computer because I already have one, but now I see the connectors are different. How can I get the old mouse to work with the new computer?**

—Determined in Denver

Easy, if you're going from PC to PC or Mac to Mac. But if your old mouse was for a Mac and you've changed to a PC, or vice versa, give it up and buy a new mouse.

But if you are staying within the PC kingdom, the solution's easy. For a couple of bucks, you can buy what's called a "serial-to-bus" mouse connector. You need it, and here's why.

Mice connect to a computer in one of two ways: Either they use a long, flat connector called a serial connector, or they use a perfectly round connector called a bus connector. If you have a mouse with one type of connector but your computer has another, this little doohickey will fix things.

Now. If you had some really ancient Macintosh (read: pre-1986), odds are that your mouse won't fit with any other Mac anyway. Plus it's really ancient! Spend a few bucks and get a new one, okay?

CHAPTER 3:
Software Secrets

Without software, your hardware would just be some giant, glorified doorstop. We're talking operating software, applications, programs, games, utilities, files, and documents—the stuff that makes your hardware worth the big bucks you spent in the first place. In this section we'll help you figure out what software you need, how to maintain it, and what to do when problems arise.

51. **My local software store lets you demonstrate some programs before you buy, but not all of them. How am I supposed to know a good software product from a bad one if they don't let me try it first?**

—In a Quandry in Connecticut

Remember the old days when record stores had booths you could go into and listen to records before you bought them? We're not that old, either. Still, it was a good idea.

But the problem with software is that once the dealer has opened the package to demonstrate it, no one will buy it. And because software is more expensive and so easy to copy—and steal, for that matter—software companies don't want to take back an open package. It's your basic Catch-22.

Still, there are lots of other ways to try before you buy. One great idea is to contact the maker of the software you're interested in and ask for a demonstration copy. This is becoming a common practice as software becomes more complex and even more expensive. When you're buying a program that will cost as much as a weekend getaway, you deserve to know something about it! Demo versions are usually crippled in some way—they can't print, or they can't save, or something like that—but they're complete enough to give you a good idea of how the program works.

> *Don't buy blind. Always check to see what the computer magazines think of the software—before you shop.*

It's always smart to check reviews in high-tech magazines too. Magazines like *PC Magazine*, *PC World*, and *Family PC* do an excellent job of comparing competing programs in depth. They're also objective sources of competitive information—more objective, certainly, than a salesperson working toward an incentive.

Of course, there's the obvious tactic of asking friends and coworkers who use the kind of software you're looking for. This may even be a necessity if you're looking for software for a specialized area. If you're a veterinarian looking for software to manage your office, for instance, your best bet is to ask your colleagues what they use. Or check your trade publications for ads. You might have to wait a long time for *PC Magazine* to review that kind of software.

Finally, there's a fourth way that we don't recommend, but it's very common. People often "borrow" software from a friend. Sure, this is one way to try out a program, but you'd better buy a legal copy if you keep using it. Remember, even though it's incredibly easy to make a copy of a program for yourself, it's stealing when you do. Creating computer software takes a lot of work from a lot of dedicated people. They deserve to get paid for their efforts. And on the purely selfish side, you'll get a lot more out of a program if you have the documentation that comes with it and if you can call tech support to get your questions answered. Plus, legitimate users get deals on upgrades when new versions come out. So do the right thing: If you use a program, buy the program.

52. **I need to get a word processor and a spreadsheet. Should I buy them separately for around $300 apiece or get one of those all-in-one "works" programs? And if I go for the all-in-one solution, will I be giving up anything important?**

—Packrat in Pomona

Nothing important. "Works" packages are comprehensive software solutions that usually include word processor, spreadsheet, painting, and database functions. The reason programs like Microsoft Works and Claris Works are so popular among home users is because they're easier to use, cheaper, faster, and require less memory than the stand-alone applications would.

Sounds great, doesn't it? If there's a catch, it's that individual works components are not as capable as their stand-alone cousins. For instance, the word processor in Microsoft Works lacks many of the fancy features you'll find in Microsoft Word. But, considering that very few people use anything but the most basic features in any program, it's not such a big disadvantage. If you know you don't need high-end features like glossaries and indexing, a works word processor might be a better choice. It's certainly capable enough for letter writing, business reports, and term papers. And the stripped-down feature set makes it infinitely easier to learn and work with.

Works programs have the advantage in another area: Because all the components are part of a single program, they work extremely well together. For example, in ClarisWorks for Windows or Macintosh, it's simple to include a chart and spreadsheet in a report, even to dress up the tables with tools from the painting program. Doing the same by combining several stand-alone applications requires a lot of skill and boatloads of patience.

As you can tell, we highly recommend works programs, particularly for new users and home applications. Leave those big programs for people who can use company time to figure them out and who can buy them on the company's dime. Even if you find out you need more power down the road, the time you've spent learning to use a works program will make it easier for you to graduate to the big boys. But we guess you'll never even need to.

Q/A

53. Is it okay to get software from a bunch of different companies or is it better to get all my programs from the same company? Because I use Windows, is there an advantage to buying only from Microsoft?

—Fickle in Frankfurt

Not really. Sure, looking to just one or two big companies for all your software is simpler in terms of tech support, but it's also extraordinarily limiting. You think it's an accident that some of the best, most innovative software comes out of little cutting-edge software start-ups? Just as in real life, it's always the risk takers who have the drive to try something new and different.

Of course, if there are two programs you use a lot—say, a word processor and a spreadsheet—it makes sense to buy a "works" or office suite package with a suite of different computer programs all in one box (see question 52). It'll save you some time and trouble when you need to put a little copy of your spreadsheet on sales projections into your report. Applications bundled together in a works package always work better together than the stand-alone versions do.

> *Buying all your software from the same company makes tech support easier, sure, but it's also terribly limiting.*

But if you know you'll be adding programs to your computer capability by capability, be discriminating about every component—and that means every single software package you buy. Buying from a respected name is generally safe, but it always pays to shop around. If you're looking to buy an interactive multimedia storybook to help your little early reader, don't just buy based on a famous name that makes or appears in it. Software is too expensive to buy based on brand alone, and the range in software quality is enormous. Some titles that look absolutely thrilling on the box may disappoint you utterly. It also works the other way around. Again, we can't stress enough how important it is for you to try before you buy whenever you can. Or, at the very least read reviews in a magazine first. There's no reason why anyone should end up with bum software.

54. I'm beginning to run out of room on my hard disk. I've seen ads for programs like Stacker that double your disk space. Do these programs do what
they say they do?

—Squeezed in Scituate

Sooner or later, we all get squeezed. It's just a fact of life. Sooner or later, everyone starts running out of room on their hard disk. But if you don't own and use
software for doubling your disk drive, "sooner" happens twice as fast.

Stacker is the most popular of the disk-compression software packages, but
they all work pretty much the same way. They increase available disk space by
changing the data on your hard disk into a smaller, tighter code that takes up
about half as much space. When you need to see the data on your screen, the
software takes the code and turns it into readable data again. (If you're really
interested in how this works, see the accompanying sidebar.) This is why some
people complain that compression slows down computer performance, but the
truth is you'll barely notice any slowdown.

Unless you're wealthy enough to afford a new hard disk every time you're old
one fills up, disk compression is a pretty good idea. There are some caveats. For
one thing, there are some files in DOS and Windows that you don't want to compress for technical reasons. Luckily, all disk-compression products let you choose
how much of the hard disk you want compressed. Most people compress
between 50 percent and 90 percent of their hard drive.

It's true compressed disks are a bit less reliable. When you store more data
in a smaller space and you're adding the extra complexity of encoding and
decoding it all the time, obviously there's a greater chance of data loss. If you
choose to compress your hard disk, make sure to back it up often. And use the
disk utilities provided with the compression software to check your hard disk's
integrity regularly.

THAT OLD BLACK MAGIC

No matter how many times the experts say there's nothing dangerous about disk
compression, a lot of people feel pretty shaky about the idea. But there's nothing
magical or strange about disk compression.

First you need to know that computers represent data in small chunks called
bytes. Each byte can contain a letter, a number, or, in the case of a drawing, a dot
on the screen. Compression programs rely on the fact that most files contain a lot
of redundant information. A picture filled with blue sky contains many hundreds
of bytes of blue. Blue-blue-blue-blue, seemingly ad infinitum. Those hundreds of

Finally, the compression routines have to run all the time, so they are always resident in your RAM when you're computer is turned on. Since RAM space is scarce—many programs require every little bit you can muster—the 40K or so allotted to compression programs might be a problem. Check your software manuals first.

55. **I just installed a Windows program that really stinks. I tried to delete it, but there still are a lot of its files all over the place. How do you uninstall a Windows program?**

—Scattered in Schenectady

How do you nail Jello to a tree? Once you install them, Windows programs are devilishly difficult to get rid of. It usually involves a lot more than just deleting the program's icon or even the subdirectory you're storing it in.

That's one of the reasons we like programs that have an "uninstaller" as well as an installer. Software companies have a hard time admitting to themselves that there might be a need for uninstalling a program, but it happens all the time.

How do you nail Jello to a tree? Windows programs, once you install them, are entirely too hard to get rid of.

But let's backtrack a minute. When you install a Windows program, you do more than just copy the program to your hard disk. Windows installers often stick files into subdirectories where Windows is residing, and maybe in other hard-to-find locations. After you've installed a few programs, it can be pretty

bytes can be reduced to two, one containing the color, another containing information on how many dots of that color are to follow.

Data compression can reduce the size of text and graphics files by half or more. Files that contain less redundancy, like programs, don't squeeze down quite as much. We find that the typical mix of programs and data squeezes down by about 70 percent. That means you can expect to get 1.7 times more disk space on a compressed drive.

difficult to figure out which files came from where. And they're literally hidden all over the place.

There are a number of programs written specifically to help you remove unused files and programs you no longer want on your hard disk, even if the software maker doesn't specifically include one in its packaging. Check your local store for programs that will scan your hard-disk drive looking for duplicate files and files that aren't being used, then offer to delete them. Some programs, such as Remove-It, will actually sit in the background during the installation process, making a note of all the changes that the installation makes to your hard drive. When you ask them to, these programs can completely reverse the installation.

We think Remove-It does the best job of uninstalling programs, but it uses up some memory, and can slow installations to a crawl as it tracks the changes that are occurring. Some other programs, such as Uninstaller, are less intrusive, but in our tests we've found that they don't remove absolutely every unused file.

56. **I've written a bunch of stuff in WordPerfect, but my boss recently said we now have to do everything in Microsoft Word. I don't have to retype all my old letters and memos now, do I?**

—Bossed in Boston

Heavens, no! People are always moving from one program to another, and in most cases there are lots of ways to take your data right along with you.

There is, for instance, a standardized way for computers to represent text and numbers, and data stored in this way is generally readable by any computer software program. It's called ASCII (pronounced *ASK-kee*), which stands for the American Standard Code for Information Interchange. Almost all modern computers use ASCII codes for text and numbers. Which means that files saved as ASCII—sometimes known as "text-only" files—can be easily transported from program to program and machine to machine without any translation.

Unfortunately, there is no ASCII standard for many of the fancy things people like to do with their text. ASCII files contain no information at all about typefaces, emphasis, spacing, margins, or any of the other formatting features that make a document look good. And every program uses different ways of representing this information. Moving files from program to program is mostly a matter of saving your file in ASCII format (most word processors will give you the option) and opening that plain old ASCII text in the new program. Then, you replace all the formatting using your new program.

Microsoft Word is unusual in that it will even read formatted files created in WordPerfect, because WordPerfect is so popular. So just open your WordPerfect files from within Word and it will make the translation automatically. That's because Word can understand most of the WordPerfect formatting codes. Occasionally some of WordPerfect's formatting is not translated correctly, but you can usually fix any imperfections with minimal effort.

Today's best programs are equipped with the ability to read many common file formats. If you're moving from a more obscure format, however, you might have to use special software that's designed to translate from one format to another. These programs focus on word processing documents, but can also translate other kinds of data, including spreadsheet and graphics file formats. On the Macintosh side we like MacLink Plus and Software Bridge. Windows users can call on a variety of utilities for their translations.

57. I'm in a mixed marriage. My wife has a Mac. I have a PC. Help save our relationship! What's the easiest way for us to set things up so we can view and use each other's documents and files?

—Mixed in Michigan

As you've no doubt already surmised, the PC and the Macintosh don't have the same disk format. The latest Macs come with a built-in program called PC Exchange, which lets the Mac read PC disks automatically. That's good news for your wife, the Mac user—you can easily copy files to and from a DOS disk. (Don't confuse this with the ability to "run" DOS programs on a Mac. We're just talking about looking at and editing documents. Mac computers still require Mac programs, and the same goes for DOS-based PCs.)

The latest Macs come with a built-in program called PC Exchange, which lets the Mac read the text files on PC disks.

Of course, you can't just stick a Mac disk into a PC and read it. However, software does exist for both PCs and older Macs without PC Exchange that can help you translate the foreign disk format. On the Windows and DOS side, a utility called MacInDOS does a good job.

We do have some good news for mixed marriages like yours: If you and your wife do a great deal of PC-to-Mac-and-back again file translation, there are more and more applications available that use the same format for both platforms. That means no translation is necessary at all. This is very handy. For example, as we write this book, one of us is writing on a Macintosh, the other on a PC running Windows, but because we are both using Microsoft Word, we can send our files back and forth and collaborate on them without translation. ClarisWorks, Claris Filemaker Pro, Microsoft Word, Microsoft Excel, Microsoft FoxPro, Pagemaker, and many other programs share identical file formats with their Mac and

PC versions. If you have to share a lot of files between computers on a regular basis, you're best off using programs like these.

58. **I feel kind of silly about this. I just finished writing a very important report and I can't find it anywhere on my computer. But I know I saved it. Now what do I do?**

—*Lost in Lexington*

If you saved it, it's there. Somewhere. It's just a matter of finding it.

Our first hard drive was a whopping 5MB. That was 15 years ago. We didn't lose many files, because there wasn't that much stuff on the drive to begin with. Today's hard drives are often 100 times bigger. That means it's hundreds of times harder to find the files you saved on it. Unless you're one of those organized types who creates folders or subdirectories for each topic and religiously files away each document in the place where it belongs, you're bound to lose a file from time to time. For many people, a hard disk is not unlike that messy junk drawer in your kitchen or den. Throwing stuff in there is the surest way to lose it later.

Avoid lost files in the first place by storing them with logical names and in logical directories.

Macintosh owners and people who use IBM OS/2 on PCs have it easier, certainly, than DOS and Windows users when it comes to tracking down lost files. That's because both the Mac and OS/2 allow people to name files using real words and names that aren't limited to 11 characters (eight characters plus a three-character extension, as in LETTER88.DOC) as DOS and Windows files are. In a Mac or in OS/2, for example, you could name that same document LETTER TO MOM - SEPT. Clearly, having a file with a plain English name makes it a lot easier to find later. Cryptic 11-character names are easy to overlook. Luckily, both DOS and Windows come with file finding features built-in, and many DOS and Windows programs you buy in the store have their own file finding functions, too. Such features typically let you type in the name of the file (if you remember it), a range of calendar dates when you might have saved it, or even individual characters or words that were in the document. Then, they search the whole hard disk or a part of it for files or parts of files that match what you're looking for.

A FILE NAME A DAY KEEPS THE HASSLES AWAY

You can go a long way towards avoiding losing files in the first place by carefully storing your documents in logical places, and by naming them in consistent ways you can remember later. In offices or homes where several people are using the same computer and creating different files on it, you might find it handy to always begin the file name with the initials of the author, and maybe even a version number, like so: GSLL001.DOC. The DOC extension is used to indicate a Microsoft Word file. Subdirectories or folders can further organize the files.

The Macintosh uses a similar structure, but with hierarchical folders, instead of subdirectories. (Subdirectories and folders are really just two different ways of looking at the same thing, anyway.)

This method makes it much easier to find files by browsing around the directories. But most of the home users we know can't be bothered to be so organized.

A typical file-organizing technique

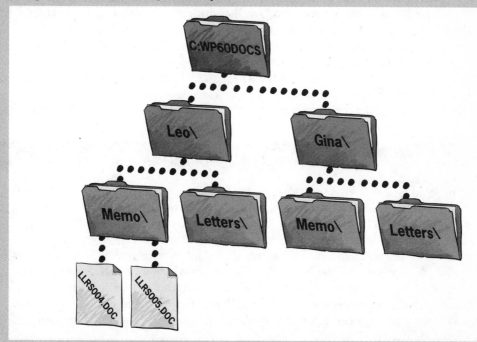

59. **My PC is acting funny. I think it might have a virus. How do I find out, and what do I do if it is a virus?**

—Quarantined in Quincy

We hear this one way too often. The minute a computer starts acting up, people shout "Virus! Virus!" but the general hysteria over computer viruses is way over-blown. Viruses aren't all that common, particularly if you don't engage in high risk behaviors like sharing disks with others. It is far more likely you've encoun-tered a recurring error (or a bug, which has nothing to do with a virus) in the soft-ware you're using.

What are computer viruses? They're small programs designed to infiltrate your computer and modify its behavior, often with destructive consequences. They sneak into your PC by piggybacking on other programs, or by hiding on floppy disks. You may not even realize your computer has been infected until much later. And almost all viruses spread themselves by hopping onto other disks and programs.

Viruses are a kind of computer vandalism, usually perpetrated by teenage hackers. Some viruses are created by disgruntled employees and are targeted at their employers. There have even been cases of viruses that were created for study by legitimate computer scientists but somehow escaped into general circu-lation. Hundreds of new computer viruses are identified every year.

As we mentioned, you don't have to worry much about getting infected by a computer virus unless you share disks with someone else. Contrary to popular belief, infection from online services almost never happens. If you do share disks,

PRACTICE SAFE COMPUTING

Virus programs do all sorts of things, some of them whimsical, some of them destructive. The most common virus of all, Stoned, acts on PCs. Once it infects your computer, you'll get the message "Your computer is now stoned" when you turn on the computer. Virus researchers believe that the Stoned virus was not intended to be harmful. As often happens, though, the virus inadvertently causes some data loss when it installs itself. The geeks who write viruses aren't the world's best programmers, so many viruses contain unplanned side effects.

Other viruses are intentionally harmful. The Michelangelo virus activates on March 6 each year. When triggered, Michelangelo will erase the entire contents of your hard-disk drive. Yikes!

Another very common virus is Cascade. When activated (usually by date) Cas-cade causes all the letters on your screen to tumble into a heap at the bottom. Cascade is harmless, but it can be quite disconcerting.

particularly with networked systems at school and work, you are at high risk. In any case, all of us should use an antivirus program to check periodically for infection. If these programs find a virus, they will alert you and offer to remove it. If you're at high risk, you might want to use a feature offered by most virus checkers that constantly monitors for infection and prevents it before it can occur.

How do antivirus programs work? Well, when a new virus is reported, virus researchers spring into action. These researchers are from universities and antivirus-software companies around the world. They analyze the virus by decoding its instructions and trying to understand what the virus is designed to do, so that they can create an innoculation to reverse its actions.

During the analysis, researchers identify a unique signature for the virus: a series of bytes that are the virus's fingerprint. Antivirus programs work by searching your hard-disk drive for those unique virus signatures. When the signature is found, the program alerts you to the possible presence of the virus. If you've got one, be sure to notify everyone you shared floppies with, so they can test their systems too. Then, run the utility inside your antivirus program that will remove the virus from your system.

Macintosh and PC users have many excellent antivirus programs to choose from. Don't think you have to spend a lot of money for protection, either. Since version 6.0, both MS-DOS and PC-DOS have come with very capable antivirus programs. They're probably all you'll need. On the Macintosh side, John Norstad's excellent Disinfectant program is absolutely free. Norstad wrote it as a public service to the Mac community—what a good guy. Look for Disinfectant on all the online services that support Macs, or get it from your local Macintosh user group. If you're willing to spend some money, you'll find a wide variety of commercial antivirus programs at your local software store. They don't seem to work any better than the free programs though. It doesn't matter where you get the program from—just get it, keep it up-to-date, and use it regularly to check your disks.

60. **I'm not the world's fastest typist. Truth is, I could probably qualify as the world's slowest. I have a real hard time using any more than two fingers, and even those two are pretty embarrassing. Is there software I can use to dictate to my computer and have it type my letters for me?**

—Need Dictation in Knoxville

This is one of the most asked-for computer applications—not surprising considering how many non-typists like you are now faced with learning how to control their computers. And luckily, typing-free computer usage is just now becoming possible. We do recommend you get a handle on your typing skills—in the long run, you'll find it a lot easier than dealing with the new dictation software on the market—but there are two kinds of solutions available.

The first kind lets you issue simple voice commands to your computer. Things like "file open," "save," and "quit." These programs may save a little typing and mouse clicking, but they really serve more as a gimmick than as a useful program. There are a number of programs that can do this, and all they require is a microphone and, for PC users, a sound card. In fact, many PC sound cards come with voice command software, so you may already have some. If you're interested in trying out voice recognition, this is an inexpensive—though not very satisfying—way to start.

You're likely to be disappointed with even the best voice-recognition software.

The second kind of voice recognition software is the kind you're is looking for. It costs a lot more, and typically requires installation of a pricey adapter card. Even so, you're likely to be disappointed with the results. Big companies like Apple and IBM have spent millions of dollars on research on dictation software. They've come up with pretty effective programs, but they require fast computers. And you'll be required to spend quite some time training the computer. The current generation of software has to learn all about your particular speech patterns before it will work. Versions that work with all voices without training are still a way off. Our advice? Learn how to type! You'll find it well worth the trouble.

61. When I turn on my Macintosh, it just sits there blinking at me. What's it waiting for, a bribe? Help.

—Blinked Out in Blacksville

When you turn on a computer, any computer, it transmogrifies from an inanimate hunk of plastic, metal, and glass into a machine that almost seems to have a personality.

But if something goes wrong at any point during this transformation, your computer will just blink at you stupidly like a grouchy old man with a hangover. It's not pleasant. A lot of things could be to blame. So let's walk through the typical start-up routine for any personal computer.

The computer start-up process is called "booting up." The term comes from the phrase "to pull yourself up by your bootstraps." That's pretty apt because as the computer "boots" it loads a succession of increasingly complex programs, each building on the earlier programs, until it has achieved full computerhood.

It all begins with a flick of the switch that sends the electricity to the computer's circuitry. Once it's all juiced-up, the computer loads its first program from a chip that the nerds call ROM, or Read Only Memory. This rudimentary program contains something called the Power-On Self-Test, or POST. (Are we acronym challenged, yet?) The POST program tests the computer's RAM chips, disks, and more, to see that it's all ready and working. On PCs this is when you'll see a message about the computer's manufacturer, the ROM's manufacturer, and a brief RAM test that counts up to the total amount of available RAM.

On Macs this is the brief pause when the screen is gray, and nothing else seems to be happening. If the computer fails the POST, it will give you some form of warning: A beep and an error code on the PC, or a black screen and a frowning Mac with an error code below it on the Macintosh. If the POST is passed with flying colors, the computer loads the operating system from the hard disk.

On Macintosh computers you'll see a smiling Macintosh to signal that all is well with the computer. If that smile turns to a blinking question mark—and that sounds like what's happening to you—it means your Mac can't find a disk with the operating system on it. If you know you have a hard disk with an operating system on it in the computer—that is, if you've successfully used this Mac before—this could be cause for alarm. Take a deep breath and try turning the machine off and on again.

For some reason, computers, like other electronic devices, just stop working for no apparent reason. If you can't get past the blinking no matter how many times you try, take that Mac to the shop. In fact, even if it does work eventually, you might want to get it checked. This kind of stuff can be hard on the nerves!

62. **I just bought Quicken to balance my checkbook. I've tried to read the manual that came with the program, but I can't understand a word of it. Is there an easier way to learn how to use it?**

—Struggling in Steuben

Before we get a nasty call from the folks at Intuit who publish Quicken, we should say that we get this question all the time about almost every program out there. Quicken has one of the best manuals in the business, but as you've discovered, even an excellent manual can seem like Greek when you're new to computing.

The problem is that manuals are supposed to be references for what features the program offers, not tutorials on how to use the program. Consider yourself lucky you're learning about computers now, and not five or ten years ago. Used to be, software came in baggies with 20 pages of photocopied instructions. Now programs come with thousands of pages of documentation in three or four volumes, and they're still hard to read!

How your computer boots up

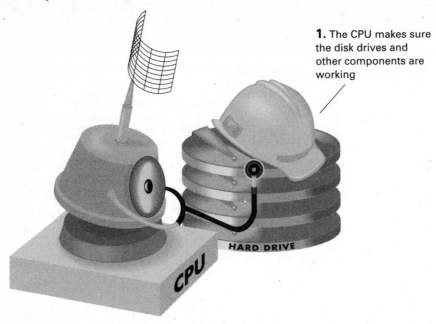

1. The CPU makes sure the disk drives and other components are working

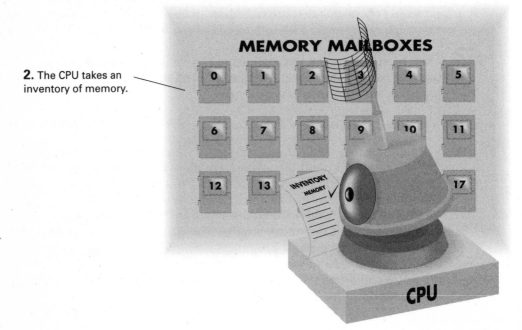

2. The CPU takes an inventory of memory.

3. The read/write head locates the operating system on the hard disk.

OPERATING SYSTEM

HARD DRIVE

4. On a Mac, a happy Macintosh face appears, followed by a Welcome to the Macintosh screen, and then the desktop. On the PC, a DOS prompt appears.

C:\>

Q/A

Of course, there are a lot of ways to learn how to use a program. Computer books on every conceivable subject proliferate. Many of them do a good job of showing you how to get the most out of your software, and are much easier to understand than the manuals. But beware, because if you have trouble learning from the manual, you may have trouble with a book, too. Many of us are visual learners. We need to see how something works before we can understand it. If this sounds like you, ask a friend for help, or attend a user's group meeting to find a friend who can show you in a couple of lessons how the software works. Magazines such as *Computer Shopper* list users groups every month.

Some people learn best through sound, so check your local bookstore for audio cassettes that put you through the paces. You can even buy tutorial videos for the most popular software. These work well for people who need to actually see how a feature works. But because the TV is rarely near the computer, videos aren't great for people who like to try things out as they learn.

Some people are visual learners: They need to see how something works before they can understand it. If this sounds like you, find a friend who can show you in a couple of examples how the software works. Then, just use the manual for reference.

Computer-based training (CBT) is all the rage these days. These are computer programs that run right along with the program you're trying to learn. The CBT software will walk you through tasks step-by-step, like a patient tutor. And the best part is that you're using the actual program you're trying to learn. Many of the more complex programs come with these software tutorials, and many more tutorials are available from third parties.

Just remember, you're not alone. Everyone has trouble figuring out how to use software. And as our computers and their programs become more complex, the problem's only going to get worse. But you'll find many people around who will be more than glad to help. After all, someone helped them get started!

63. I tried to install a new game, but when I run it my PC shows a message that says I'm out of memory. How do I add more memory to my computer?

—Maxed in Manhasset

Adding more memory to a PC is pretty easy, but you may not need to. When you get "out of memory" error messages, more often than not you just need to better manage the memory you've already got. It's sort of like when you finally get

Q/A

around to folding the clothes in your dresser drawers, you seem to have so much more space. Memory management works in much the same way.

In most cases, what the program is really trying to tell you is that you're out of a particular kind of memory known as "conventional memory." In a PC, that means you've run out of space in the first 640K of RAM, which is the only memory DOS and DOS applications can use. Windows applications can use more than that—up to 16MB in fact—but that extra real estate is known as "extended memory."

Even if you have many megabytes (or even gigabytes) of extended memory, you can never have more than 640K of conventional memory. And you'll almost always have somewhat less since your system probably loads several small programs into conventional memory when you start up.

These memory munchers include disk-caching software, and programs that tell your computer how to access CD-ROM drives, sound cards, networks, and more. Once the memory munchers are loaded, a typical multimedia PC may only have 500K of conventional memory left to run regular programs.

> *You may not need to add more memory. Even when you get "out of memory" error messages, more often than not, you just need to better manage the memory you've already got.*

Since accessing conventional memory is much faster than accessing extended memory, most DOS programs want as much conventional memory as possible. Games are the biggest memory hogs, so your problem is pretty common. Fact is, 500K isn't even enough to play many of today's games. When you try to run one of these piggy programs you'll get an "out of memory" error.

There are two things you can do to make enough room for this game to run. (Check your game manual for more specific details. This is such a common problem that most DOS games come with detailed instructions on how to get them running.)

Plan A: Use a memory manager.   Ever since Microsoft released version 5.0, DOS has come with a memory manager. This is a program that increases available conventional memory by moving all those little memory munchers like disk caches, CD-ROM drivers, and the like into an area above conventional memory called "high memory." If you've got DOS 5.0 or later running on a 386 or better, you can automatically install the memory manager by typing MEMMAKER at the DOS prompt.

MEMMAKER does a good job of recovering memory, but if you still don't have enough to run that DOS game, you might want to buy a commercial memory manager. We like Netroom from Helix software and QEMM by Quarterdeck. These programs are more aggressive than MEMMAKER about finding places to stash the memory munchers, but they can cause compatibility problems. Some

Q/A

games won't work when a memory manager is running. When that happens you'll have to switch to Plan B.

Plan B: Change your start-up configuration. If the program you want to run doesn't require some of the memory munchers you normally load, like the CD-ROM drivers, disk cache, network, and so on, you can disable them and recover the conventional memory they take up. Usually the easiest way to do this is to create a "boot disk." You'll start the computer from this disk instead of the hard drive.

You create a boot disk by formatting a blank floppy using the command FORMAT A: /S. Then copy the files CONFIG.SYS and AUTOEXEC.BAT from your hard disk to the floppy. Finally, use the DOS Editor, EDIT, to modify those files on the floppy and remove unnecessary entries. We recommend this procedure only to people who know what they're doing. Many of the entries in the CONFIG.SYS and AUTOEXEC.BAT files are obscure. It's not always easy to know what to change. Some games can automatically create a boot disk for you. That's a feature we think all memory-hungry DOS games should offer.

DOS's restriction on the amount of memory your programs can access is a legacy of the original IBM PCs. In the next few years we should see new operating systems that eliminate this hereditary curse and let programs access every bit of the RAM you have in your machine. It's about time. Let's hope this is one question we won't have to answer in the future.

If you're using Windows or a Macintosh, an "out of memory" error message has an entirely different meaning. Both these operating systems are able to access the entire memory pool, so if you get an error it's likely that you really *are* out of RAM. You can fix this in the short term by turning on virtual memory from the control panel—that is, by using the extra space on your hard disk as RAM—but it's very slow. If you run out of memory a lot, it might be time to invest in some additional RAM for your machine.

THANKS FOR THE MEMORY

The original IBM PC came with 16K of RAM, expandable to 64K. Back in 1981, its designers felt that was sufficient. But they weren't stupid.

They knew that as the years passed people would write bigger programs that needed more RAM, so they designed a lot of headroom into the specification. They made space in the machine for up to 1MB of RAM. That was the maximum that the original PC's CPU, the Intel 8088, could access. As much as 640K of that memory would be made available to programs.

The remaining memory would be reserved for the display screen, add-in cards, and other hardware. No program, they reasoned, would ever need more than 640K of memory. Boy were they wrong.

When companies began using Intel's more sophisticated CPUs in their

Macintosh users might try a less expensive software solution to memory short-ages called RAM Doubler. For less than $100, RAM Doubler tricks your Mac into thinking it has twice the memory. Although there are occasional compatibility problems, RAM Doubler is a great way to get more memory.

64. **Every once in a while when I'm using a particular program I get the error message "General Protection Fault" and the computer stops working. What is a General Protection Fault, and what can I do about it?**

—Busted in Biloxi

Your system isn't busted, Busted, it's crashed. A General Protection Fault, or GPF, is the kind of system error you get when Microsoft Windows gets confused and freezes up. On the Macintosh you might see the error message "An error of Type 1 has occurred." In DOS you probably won't see any error message at all—the com-puter will just stop working. All computer programs crash at some point—even programs advertised as "crash-proof."

It's unfortunate, but even the best programs aren't perfect. Crashes happen when a program does something it's not supposed to, like change an area of memory that belongs to another program, or try to divide a number by zero (that's impossible, of course), or attempt to take over your computer on its road to world domination (this almost never happens). Most commercial programs contain hundreds of thousands of instructions, and are written by huge teams of programmers. The level of complexity is so breathtakingly high, and there's so much going on behind the scenes, that it's almost impossible to create an error-free program.

machines, the amount of RAM that could be accessed went up. The 80286 can address up to 16MB of memory. The 80386 and 486 can address up to a whopping four billion bytes (4 gigabytes) of RAM! But here's the catch: DOS still can't access more than 1MB. In their zeal to preserve compatibility with older programs, Microsoft has never increased that limit.

So how does your PC access more than 1 MB of RAM? By tricking the com-puter into thinking that everything's in that original 640K of memory. When data stored outside that area is needed, it's swapped into the lower 640K before DOS notices. That slows the computer down slightly. So programmers who need performance try to keep as much of the program as they can in the origi-nal 640K of memory.

Software companies do what they can to reduce the number of bugs. They will commonly send prerelease versions of software, called "beta" versions, to a select group of users for testing. And every big software company has a quality assurance team whose main job is to bang on the company's software until it breaks. But no matter what companies do, there'll be at least a few errors, or "bugs" as they're called by programmers, left hanging around to bite you when you least expect it.

The severity of a program's bugs can range from completely innocuous to annoying to downright serious. Sometimes bugs will trigger an error message, like the GPF message that started this discussion. Once you get a serious error message like a GPF, you should attempt to save whatever you're working on, exit out of Windows, and restart your machine.

Most often, a GPF is a prelude to what's known as a "hard crash." That's when everything stops working, including the keyboard and mouse, and you're forced to reset the machine by pressing the reset button, or turning off the power, waiting a few seconds, and turning it back on again. This clears everything out of memory and starts you with a clean slate.

Always write down any computer message you see—you'll need them if you end up calling tech support—but try not to read too much into them. Usually it's just the computer's best guess as to what's wrong. And computers, as we're learning, aren't very good guessers!

65. **I just added Windows to DOS and the system seems so slow. Is this normal? How do I make Windows run faster?**

—Sluggish in Savannah

This is a common complaint from people who've switched from DOS to Windows. Because Windows uses graphics, rather than just letters and numbers on screen, it moves slower. Sure, Windows applications are much easier to use than plain DOS ones, but it takes a lot more CPU, hard disk, memory, and graphics power to run Windows than it does to run DOS.

Which leads us to what we call Gina and Leo's Power Paradox: The newer you are to computers, the more powerful a computer you need. If you want to use a graphical user interface like Windows, you'll have a need for speed in two areas.

First, you'll need fast video electronics to put all that data on the screen in a timely fashion. You can speed up Windows quite a bit by replacing your old video card with a Windows accelerator card. These cards contain special circuitry to speed up the kinds of drawing operations Windows programs use most. Newer computers intended to run Windows are being built with fast video circuitry called "local bus video." If you're buying a new PC, look for one with local bus. It'll increase your Windows performance by as much as 2,000 percent.

Q/A

Second, you'll want a fast processor to do all the calculations necessary to draw the graphics on the screen. We don't recommend running Windows on anything less than a 486 microprocessor. You'll also want lots of fast disk storage because graphical programs are larger. Buy at least a 340MB hard disk. And you'll need more memory for the same reason, at least 8MB of RAM.

Remember, when it comes to computers, easy-to-use means you need lots of power. Don't try to use a graphical user interface like Windows on a machine from the DOS ages.

BIT-MAPPED VS. CHARACTER-BASED

The technical difference between Windows and DOS really boils down to the fact that Windows is a "bit-mapped" environment and DOS is "character-based" one. In a bit-mapped display, the computer's screen is drawn dot by dot. Character-based displays draw a screen letter by letter. A character-based display is much faster, but much more limited in terms of what it can display on screen.

The biggest advantage of a bit-mapped display is that software can draw pictures on it. Without the ability to draw pictures, we wouldn't have icons, windows, menus, fonts, and all the other features that make a Windows-based PC or a Macintosh easy to use. These features make up what's known as a "Graphical User Interface," or "GUI" (pronounced *gooey*) for short. GUIs make it so much easier to learn and use a computer. Once you're used to graphics, text-based interfaces look positively primitive.

Until 1984, all computer displays were character based. That's when Apple introduced the Macintosh, the first personal computer with a bit-mapped display. The Macintosh begat Windows and Windows begat OS/2, and pretty soon no one wanted to use a character-based screen any more.

Character-based computer screens are divided into grids 80 characters wide and 24 characters tall. Each cell in that grid can contain one letter or number. An entire screen takes only 80×24 or 1,920 bytes of memory.

Now compare that with our modern bit-mapped VGA display. It's 640 dots wide, 480 lines tall, and each dot can contain any of 256 colors. That screen takes up 307,200 bytes of memory.

In the days when a computer was maxed out at 65,536 bytes of memory, it would have been unthinkable to reserve more than four times that amount for the screen display. And the microprocessors of that time weren't nearly fast enough to pump that much data onto the screen.

So it wasn't until computers got powerful enough that computer designers could give us the easy-to-use GUI. Unfortunately, if you're trying to use a GUI on an underpowered system, it really will seem like you're working in goo.

Q/A

66. **I've heard it said that using a disk cache will speed up my computer. I know I have 256K processor cache. Is that enough?**

—Cache Poor in Coral Gables

You're confusing caches! That's easy to do. So let's explain what a cache is, and then talk about the two different kinds of cache in your computer.

In general, a cache (pronounced *cash*) is an area of memory reserved to save already-used information in case it's wanted again. There are several different kinds of caches, including processor cache, which helps your CPU work faster, and disk cache, which helps your hard disk move faster. We recommend processor caches for PCs and disk caches for all computers.

How a disk cache works

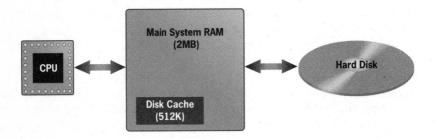

The idea behind cache is that your computer usually asks for the same piece of information again and again. Since data can be accessed from memory much more quickly than from your disk drive, caching recently accessed information can really speed things up.

A disk cache takes up some of your RAM to store recently accessed data from the hard disk. MS-DOS and Windows come with very good disk cache software called SmartDrive. We say install SmartDrive if you haven't done so already. Your DOS manual will tell you how. You can buy faster disk caches from other companies, but SmartDrive is more than enough for most people.

SmartDrive reserves some of your system's memory for the cache—you tell it how much. Microsoft recommends that you set your SmartDrive cache to 1,024K if you have 4–7MB of RAM, 2,048K for 8–10MB of RAM, and 4,096K for systems with more than 10MB of RAM.

Macintosh computers come with disk caches built into the system. Use the Memory control panel to set the size of your disk cache. Because of the way the Mac file system works, Macintoshes don't benefit as much from a disk cache, but you should use it anyway. Allow 32K of disk cache for each megabyte of memory in your machine, up to 512K of cache. Some Macintosh programs like Photoshop do their own caching. If you use Photoshop a lot, turn the cache down to 32K.

Hardware disk caches are available for both the Mac and PC. Hardware caches have their own built-in memory, so they don't take up any of your RAM, but they're expensive and the average user won't see much increase in speed.

That's disk cache. Processor cache is the same, but different. Processor cache is very fast memory used to store instructions your CPU has recently executed. It makes a big difference in how fast your computer runs. There are two kinds of processor cache, internal and external. Internal processor cache is part of the chip's design and cannot be increased by the user. The Intel 486 and Motorola 68040, for example, have 8K of processor cache built in.

External, or level 2, processor cache is usually installed into the computer during its manufacture. The RAM used for processor caches is very costly because it's very fast—four times faster than your regular RAM, so it's outrageously expensive to upgrade your processor cache. That's one reason why manufacturers sometimes build computers without processor cache. Even though these computers cost less, you pay the price in poor performance. We don't recommend buying any PC with less than 256K external processor cache. If your machine has more than 16MB of memory, get 512K of processor cache.

For some reason, most Macintosh computers don't come with external processor cache. That's not to say they can't benefit from it. People who really want to get the most out of their Macs often add external processor cache cards.

It can take some extra cash to get enough cache, but it's worth it.

67. **Oops. I accidentally erased the only copy of my wedding guest list. I really don't want to type this in again. Is there any way to get it back? I think my mother-in-law is going to kill me!**

—Lovelorn in Lancaster

Good news! If you act fast, the wedding can go on as planned.

When you erase a file on Macs and PCs, you don't really erase the information in the file. At least not right away. You are merely changing its entry in the catalog of files maintained by the disk operating system.

The operating system marks that space as available, but doesn't go so far as to actually delete any data. If you act before any other file takes that space, you can get your deleted file back intact. A man named Peter Norton made $300 million exploiting that fact. (And you made fun of nerds in school.)

About 12 years ago, a friend came to Peter begging for help. She'd done much the same thing as you and was desperate to recover her data. Peter sat down and wrote a quick utility to restore the file's catalog entry, and the file magically reappeared. He named the program "UnErase." UnErase was followed by a series of other handy disk utilities that were christened "The Norton Utilities," and an empire was created.

> *When you erase a file on Macs and PCs, you don't really erase the information in the file. At least not right away. You are merely changing its entry in the catalog of files maintained by the disk operating system.*

When Peter sold The Norton Utilities to the Symantec Corporation he retired and became an art collector. But his programs are still sold by Symantec, and they still collect raves. Every computer owner should own a copy of The Norton Utilites or a product like it. And when the day comes that you accidentally erase an irreplaceable file, you'll thank your lucky stars you read this book.

You may kiss the groom.

68. I saw an ad for IBM's Warp operating system on a football game this afternoon. They said it was a better DOS than DOS, and a better Windows than Windows. Well, I use DOS with Windows now. What does Warp add to the situation, and how do I know it will still run my Windows software?

—Fan in Fairmont

Did you ever think a company as conversative and buttoned-down as IBM would come up with a product name like Warp? Neither did we, but there you have it. Old Tommy Watson must be spinning in his grave.

Warp is being heavily advertised as a powerful new operating system for the millions of people who use DOS and Windows programs. And like any choice in the computer biz, it has plusses and minuses.

OS/2 Warp is the latest version of an IBM-made operating system called OS/2. Previous, more drearily named versions you may have heard of are OS/2 1.0, 2.0, and 2.1. Like DOS, OS/2 Warp is an operating system in the sense that it can perform all the basic operations your computer needs for managing resources and storing and accessing files. But unlike DOS, OS/2 is able to use the advanced features of 386 and 486 computers to run multiple copies of DOS and Windows.

That's why OS/2 can run Windows programs, as well as DOS programs and OS/2 programs, and why OS/2 is especially good at what the geeks call "multitasking."

Multitasking simply means running more than one task or program at a time. For instance, you might want to copy a bunch of files to a floppy while you're downloading e-mail. Because OS/2 was designed from the get-go to do this, it does a much better job of multitasking than DOS, Windows, or even the Mac. And because OS/2 is so good at keeping track of lots of things going on at once, it doesn't crash as often.

Also, OS/2—unlike DOS—takes advantage of memory management features in the 386 and later computers, so it can access all the memory (up to 4 gigabytes) in your machine without complicated memory management software. DOS, remember, can only look at 640K of memory at once.

> *Unlike DOS, OS/2 uses advanced features of the 386 and 486 chips that allow it to run multiple copies of DOS and Windows at once.*

There is one thing we don't like about Warp—it's not as well supported by software and hardware companies as DOS-based Windows. Here's why: As of this writing, IBM has only sold about six million copies of all versions of OS/2 (including Warp), compared to the over 60 million copies of Windows in circulation. Now six million is nothing to sneeze at, but software makers are interested in the widest possible audience. When you go to the store, you'll find many more choices in Windows software than in programs written specifically for OS/2.

A bigger problem with OS/2 Warp is that hardware makers are kind of slow in getting warped. That means some peripherals, like CD-ROM drives or video displays, may not work well, or at all, with Warp. IBM has been trying very hard to reverse this situation by enticing more developers to join the team, and they are getting there, but the fact remains that Warp doesn't work on as many IBM-PC compatibles as Windows and DOS do. It's a big problem. If you want to get Warped, we suggest you check with your computer manufacturer and component makers to make sure that they support OS/2.

If all you do is run Windows programs, Warp is not a good choice anyway. It won't run Windows programs quite as quickly as Windows itself. But if you want to run mostly DOS or OS/2 programs—or if you want to run them *and* multitask them with a few Windows programs thrown in here and there, Warp is your best bet.

69. When I watch video from my CD-ROM drive it looks like a badly-dubbed Japanese movie—and it sounds worse than a cat in a bathtub. Is this what multimedia's all about?

—Disappointed in Dayton

So what were you expecting, the Jetsons? Today's tiny, tinny video and overpriced, underdeveloped CD-ROM titles wouldn't impress Astro, much less Elroy. But that's the standard today. Could it be that the hype surrounding multimedia has outpaced the computer industry's ability to deliver? Bingo.

Don't despair though. Two things are happening now to improve the situation. First off, sound quality is improving steadily as more and more multimedia makers write titles that use CD-quality sound (known as "16-bit audio"), rather than the AM-radio–quality sound of the common 8-bit sound cards. Also, many multimedia PC makers are now opting to include quality, self-amplified speakers with their systems—a big improvement over the cheesy little speakers most have shipped with until now.

Unfortunately, the video problems are a little stickier. Even today's fastest 486 and Pentium computers aren't going to be powerful enough to display TV-quality, full-screen graphics on your monitor without a lot of assistance. And by assistance, we either mean thousands of dollars worth of hard-disk space or darned good video compression circuitry—or both.

Data compression is the real issue. As you can see from the accompanying sidebar, the chief problem with putting good video on your computer screen is the amount of data that has to be transferred from the CD-ROM or hard disk to your screen. Plus, video takes an enormous amount of hard-disk space—five minutes of

VIDEO MATH 101

Think about what it takes to display full-motion video on a computer screen, the kind of video we've been watching on TV since the Eisenhower administration. First you've got to get the picture from the CD-ROM to the screen. Our screen is 640 dots wide by 480 lines high. Each dot requires three bytes of color information. That's 900,000 bytes, or 900K, of data for every single frame of video. To turn those frames fast enough to get live-motion video, we've got to update—or repaint that screen with 900K of data behind it—60 times per second.

We'll do the math for you: that's 52MB of data per second! And we haven't even added a sound track yet. The best CD-ROM drives on the market can only manage a meager 600K per second. No wonder we've got postage stamp-sized screens, flickery pictures, and tinny sound! And it's a wonder we've even got those!

full-screen video can take up a whopping 16 gigabytes of hard-disk space. Compression software takes all those gigs of data and squeezes them down to a manageable size.

Early compression technologies could only reduce images by a factor of four. We'll soon see techniques that go much farther, reducing the video data to 1/64th its original size. That's enough to give us full-motion video and CD-quality video from today's hard-disk drives.

Can't wait? Then invest in an adapter card capable of doing on-the-fly MPEG (pronounced *EM-peg*) decompression. MPEG playback cards cost under $500. They work with specially encoded multimedia titles—games, movies, and music videos mostly—to give you full-screen video that looks almost as good as the picture from your VCR. We think that's a lot of money to spend for a limited selection of titles, though. And these cards only offer playback. The hardware it takes to *make* MPEG encoded video is way out of the price range of anyone except maybe Ted Turner, so don't expect to be storing your home videos on your hard disk anytime soon.

In the meantime, regular old PCs and Macs are getting faster all the time, so it won't be long before inexpensive high-quality video playback is widely available. Pentium-based systems are being designed specifically for video playback, with wider pathways for the data to travel and more powerful processors to speed the data along. To a great degree, the demand for high-quality video, for both business and entertainment, is driving the entire computer industry. In the next few years fast systems and improved compression techniques will turn our computer screens into full-blown smart TV sets.

Of course, by then George Jetson and the gang will be calling today's tiny, tinny videos "the golden age of multimedia." Count on it.

70. **The manual says that if the computer stops working I should press the reset button. What is the reset button? What will happen when I press it?**

—Trigger Happy in Trenton

Every computer user needs some way of restarting the machine from time to time. Turning it off and then back on again is sometimes the only way out of a sticky situation. A reset button is simply a computer manufacturer's way of making the process more convenient. Sad, isn't it?

Resetting and rebooting the system is necessary because when a program error occurs (and they inevitably do), it can stop your machine dead in its tracks. Everything stops working—an event colorfully called a "system crash" or sometimes a "system bomb." Symptoms of system crashes vary—your mouse might stop working, on the Mac a little bomb might appear, or sometimes the screen might begin to jump around and the computer will sputter like a 1954 Ford on its last legs. No matter. When your system crashes, you'll know it. And if you ever want to get back to work, you're going to have to restart it.

Q/A

In fact, if you even suspect a crash is about to occur, you should probably go ahead and restart it. Sometimes a system only half crashes and you can exit out of whatever program you're using. Maybe you'll even think you can continue working. But don't trust your machine. If it's acting weird, or if you get any strange error messages, restart it just to be safe. Once the system gets corrupted, you can't be sure what's happening to your work. So save it, and get out of there already!

> *Don't trust your machine. If it's acting weird, or if you get any strange-sounding error messages, restart your computer just to be safe.*

There are several ways to restart a computer. There's the reset button you asked about—which is alternately known, depending on the circles you travel in, as a "cold boot" or a "one-fingered salute." This is opposed to the famous "three-fingered salute"—that's when you press the Ctrl, Alt, and Del keys at the same time. Hitting that key combo is called a "warm boot"—it will reboot the computer the same way the reset button does, except it's faster.

A warm boot also isn't as complete as a cold boot—it simply reloads the operating system and starts over, whereas a cold boot, or reset, restarts everything, including all the hardware. In most cases, try the warm boot before resorting to the more stressful hard boot. And always save your work if you can before you do either. Rebooting the computer will clear all your work out of memory. (See the following chart for instructions.)

PC Users	Macintosh Users
1. Save your work and exit all running programs (if you can).	**1.** Save your work and exit all running programs (if you can).
2. Exit Windows (if you can).	**2.** Select "Shut Down" from the Finder's Special menu. (if you can, otherwise press the Reset Button.)
3. Once you see the DOS prompt, wait a second, then press Ctrl+Alt+Del to perform a warm boot.	
4. The second the screen comes back to life after the warm boot, press the reset button.	

To sum up: If you have to restart the computer, try hitting the keys Ctrl+Alt+Del first. It's less stressful on your hardware then resorting to turning your computer off and back on again with a switch.

That's because a cold boot restarts the machine no matter what it's doing, even if it's currently writing data to the hard disk. Turn your computer off when that's happening and you risk randomly spewing bits of data all over the hard disk. This, as you might imagine, is not good.

If your machine does not respond to the Ctrl+Alt+Del "three-fingered salute," only then is it safe to press the reset button. Make it a rule.

71. Why don't the fonts on my printouts look as good as they did on my screen?

—Jagged in Jericho

Sorry, Jagged, but you're using the wrong kind of typeface. It's an easy mistake. The problem is that you're printing with a typeface designed for your screen, not your printer. And though it may not make much sense, they are different.

Have you heard the term "what you see is what you get"? It's not just an old Flip Wilson routine, it's also the way computer techies describe a screen display that closely matches the printed output. We abbreviate it WYSIWYG (pronounced *whizzy-wig*). A WYSIWYG display is required for desktop publishing—otherwise how could you fix up a layout of your newsletter or magazine page? But even if you just write letters with your computer, it's great to know what the letter's going to look like on the printed page.

To get WYSIWYG, you need to use specially designed "scalable" typefaces. These are fonts designed to look good both in print and on the screeen. Both Macintosh and Windows computers come with TrueType, the most popular scalable font technology. If you want your printouts to look as good as your screen displays, use TrueType fonts in all your documents.

How can you tell if you're using a TrueType font? In Windows, check the Fonts Control Panel. While you've got it open, you can also click the TrueType button and check the box that says "Show Only TrueType Fonts in Applications." When you do, your programs will only let you use TrueType fonts, and you won't have the printing problem ever again.

Macintosh owners may have a little harder time finding out what kind of fonts they're using. Almost all current Mac fonts have been converted to True-Type, but you may have some older fonts on your system that don't print as well. Trial and error will tell. At least now, if you get jagged printing you'll know why.

Additionally, the Mac will automatically substitute printer fonts for screen fonts when printing. When you create a document using New York, for example, it will print out as Times. Slight differences between the two fonts make true WYSIWYG impossible, so if your layout is important, use a printer font whenever you're creating a document you plan to print.

MORE ON WYSIWYG

WYSIWYG—getting your monitor to show your text and graphics in the same way they'll print out—is a tricky thing to accomplish. That's because the resolution of your screen is very different from your printer's resolution. Most screens display around 72 dots per inch (DPI). On the other hand, ink-jet and laser printers can print at 300 DPI or more, which makes type appear a lot clearer and sharper.

To achieve WYSIWYG, you could take the screen image and magnify it to four times the size to get roughly 300 DPI, but the results would be pretty ugly. The letter R looks smooth, but look up close and you'll see that the diagonals have jagged, stair-stepped edges. These are called "jaggies." The higher the resolution (the finer the dots you use to draw the diagonal line), the less you'll notice the jaggies.

Font resolution and the "jaggies"

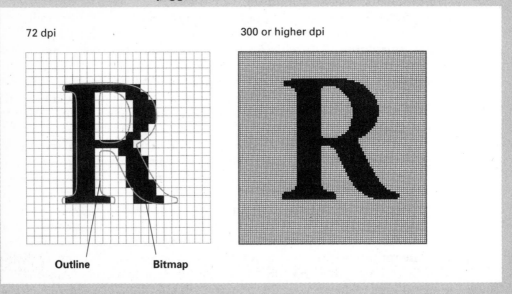

72 dpi

300 or higher dpi

Outline   Bitmap

Now, we all tolerate a certain amount of jaggedness on our computer monitors. The slight blurring effect of the CRT helps reduce the impact of the jaggies. And, frankly, we're used to it. On the other hand, we're also very used to crisp, clean print on the page. Fortunately, with laser printers you won't notice much jaggedness unless you examine the letters with a magnifying glass. But when you print a letter in a font designed for a low-resolution screen on a high-resolution printer, the jaggedness of the letters is noticeable, and annoying. And Jagged, that's what's happening to you.

Q/A

72. What's a RAM disk?

—Dizzy in Des Moines

As you already know, RAM is your computer's memory. (If you don't already know that, review the Introduction.) And you know that those little RAM chips work worlds faster than a regular hard disk, which is where all your files and programs are stored.

Well, some genius figured out how to trick PCs and Macs into treating a small portion of RAM as disk storage, which dramatically speeds up file access. You can tell your operating system to set aside a portion of your system memory and treat it as a disk drive.

This is really only a good idea if you have 16MB or more of RAM in your system. Less than that, and Windows won't have an adequate amount of memory to work with. And even then, RAM disks can't be very big—memory is expensive, after all. But there are a few situations where a RAM disk makes sense.

If you're using a laptop, for example, one of the main drains on power is the spinning hard-disk drive. Turn that disk drive off, and you'll be running your laptop minutes, if not hours, longer. If you can fit the programs and documents you'll be working on into a RAM disk, you won't need to access the hard disk. Let's say you're on a long-distance flight. You've got six hours ahead of you to work on a key report, but only three hours of battery life on your laptop. If you create a RAM disk big enough to hold your word processor and report, you can turn off your hard drive and get an extra hour or two out of your batteries.

If you have a PC with a lot of memory, you might want to create a RAM disk with the excess and use it as your TEMP drive. Many PC programs use the hard disk to store temporary files that will be deleted when the program exits. Check the following tip to see how to use a RAM disk as a scratch disk.

The most important thing to remember with a RAM disk is that its contents disappear when your turn off the power. If you're using it to save important documents, make sure to copy the documents to the hard disk before you turn off the computer.

TIP

PC owners, you can tell DOS and Windows what drive to use for temporary storage by typing **SET TEMP=x:** at the DOS prompt, or by putting this instruction into your AUTOEXEC.BAT file, a batch file of commands that are executed automatically when you turn your machine on. For example, if you create a RAM disk named D:, SET TEMP=D:, will tell programs to use the RAM disk for scratch space. Since RAM is much faster than a hard disk, this technique may speed up your programs.

---

73. **I'd like to use my computer to edit my home movies. Can I do it without spending an arm and a leg?**

—Chattanooga Cheapskate

If you read our discussion of multimedia computers a few questions back (see question 68), you'll remember that we said playing back video on today's PCs leaves a lot to be desired. Well, it's even worse if you want to use your PC to *record* your home videos.

First, you'll need to get the video into the computer, that's called digitizing because you're turning your pictures and sound into the digits that computers can understand. One minute of digitized video will run from 5MB to 3GB, depending on the screen size and quality you're looking for. You'll need a very big hard disk to do anything but the shortest videos. You'll also need some hardware to do the digitizing. These are called "video capture boards," and they can run you anywhere from $250 to $5,000 and more. The cheaper boards don't do a very good job to say the least. Once you get the video into your computer, you'll need some software to do the editing. There are a number of good programs out there for both Mac and PC. (We like Premiere from Adobe.) Expect to spend around $500.

You'll need a very big hard disk—a gigabyte or more—to edit anything but the shortest home videos.

If you want to do full-screen, full-motion video like you see on TV, you can do it but get ready to spend $15,000. Sounds like a lot, but if you consider that this kind of editing capability costs TV stations hundreds of thousands of dollars, 15 grand is a steal. A number of video professionals, including ESPN2, MTV, and many local TV stations, use the Apple Professional Video system.

Is $15,000 is out of your range? Well, you can do desktop video for considerably less, providing you're willing to settle for postage stamp-sized pictures that flicker like an old kinescope. Well, we're being a little negative here. Leo actually uses this stuff to make homemade videos of his daughter for Grandma. But it's still strictly for the hobbyist. The good news is that hardware is always getting faster and cheaper, and the day's not far off when we'll have an entire video production suite in our computers. It's just not today.

74. I'm collecting newspaper articles on Albania for a school project. Is there any way I can use the computer to keep track of them without typing them in?

—Trying to Study in Sebastapol

Sure. You need something called a scanner.

The scanner is a digitizing device—we've already talked about two other digitizing devices: the sound board and the video capture card. Digitizers turn the sights and sounds of the real world into digits the computer can understand and manipulate.

You use a scanner to copy a picture into your computer. The picture can be of anything, even a page of text. In fact, scanning text is one of the most common uses for these devices. The scanner takes a picture of the text, and then special optical character recognition (OCR) software is used to translate the *picture* of text into *real* text you can edit on your computer.

Because there's such a huge variety of typefaces, OCR software is seldom 100 percent accurate in its translation. These programs do better with large, clear type. They're not so hot with newspaper-sized print, and they're really bad with faxes. Nevertheless, in many cases you can get enough of the text to make scanning worthwhile.

For projects like yours, we recommend software like Caere's PageKeeper that keeps both the picture of the page and the OCR-translated text. That way if there's a question you can refer back to the original scan.

75. Do I need to be a programmer to use my computer?

—Scared in Sheboygan

Not at all! In the earliest days you did indeed need to be a programmer to use computers, just as you needed to be a mechanic to drive a car at the turn of the century. But as computers have become more sophisticated, and the quantity and variety of off-the-shelf software has improved, the situation has changed.

Now only a very small percentage of computer users ever program in the traditional sense.

In one sense, though, we all still program our computers. We give them instructions that we expect them to carry out, whether we're typing commands, selecting functions from a menu, or even pushing a button on the mouse. In many cases word processing, spreadsheet, and database programs come with simple programming languages called "macro languages."

You certainly don't need to know how to use macro languages to run the software, but advanced users can employ them to automate repetitive tasks. So even though you don't have to be a programmer to use a computer, as you become more adept at computing, you may find that you've become one in spite of yourself.

And that's not all bad. Some of the nicest nerds we know are computer programmers!

CHAPTER 4:
Time to Go
Online!

A computer without a modem is like an island without a bridge. Or a TV without an antenna. Or a book without a publisher, which is what this will be if we don't get on with it. So without further ado, here are some things you should know about using your computer to communicate with the outside world.

76. **My computer came with a modem and some software to use it. The only trouble is, I don't know what a modem is, or what I can do with it.**

—Ignorant in Idaho

Your modem is the key that will unlock all the power of your computer. Or to put it less poetically, and more accurately, a modem connects your computer to a telephone line so you can call other computers.

Why would you want your computer to call other computers? Well, that's what you're about to find out. There's a whole world of amazing things out there, everything from encyclopedias to cross-country gaming, from software you can download to people you can fall in love with. And all it takes is a little hardware (your modem) and a little software (a telecommunications program).

Modems work by turning the digital data stream coming out of your computer into sound that can be transmitted over regular telephone wires. That's called "modulating." And they also do the reverse, "demodulating" the sound that comes in over the phone into data your computer can understand. That's where the word modem comes from—a modem MOdulates and DEModulates data.

You connect a modem to your computer in one of two ways: via a cable attached to your computer's modem connector—that's called an external modem—or by adding a circuit board inside your computer—that's called an internal modem.

> *Modems work by turning the digital stream of data in your computer into sound waves that can travel over regular telephone lines. A modem connects your computer to phone lines, in other words, so it can call other computers.*

Once you've connected your modem, you control it by using telecommunications software. Some of the places you're going to call will have their own special software for you to use to dial in. America Online is an example. Other places work fine with a generic telecommunications program. You'll find a variety of these generic packages in your software store. Many modems come with rudimentary telecom software. Once you get "online" you'll find a wide variety of free or inexpensive software to use with your modem.

77. Are all modems alike? Is it important to buy a recognized brand name? What's the difference between expensive and inexpensive modems?

—Discerning in Denver

Don't buy just any modem. There really are differences between brands. And the best modem isn't always the best known, or the most expensive.

It's tempting to think that if you've seen one modem, you've seen them all. Modems all do about the same thing, true, but there is a big difference in how well they do it. And it's impossible to tell how good a modem is by looking at it.

Before you buy a modem, get recommendations from friends and check the reviews in magazines. We can't emphasize this enough. We've also found that a great source for modem reviews is the people who run bulletin board systems (BBSs). Not only do they really put their own modems to the test, but they have a very good idea which modems have trouble going online. If you can, ask some BBS operators for recommendations.

Modems are categorized by speed and features. The slowest modems you can buy today transfer data at 2,400 bits per second (bps). That's the equivalent of about 40 words per minute, which is somewhat slower than a good typist. The fastest modems on the market send data at a blistering 28,800 bps, or 28.8 kilo-bits per second (kbps). That's the equivalent of an entire typed page per second, which is about as fast as standard telephone lines can go. These speed ratings are maximums, by the way. A modem can travel at any speed lower than its top rated speed, too. So a 28.8 kbps modem can communicate with a 14,400, 9,600, or 2,400 bps modems when necessary.

All modems send and receive data so that you can communicate online, but some modems have more advanced features. Many of the modems on the market also have the ability to send and receive faxes. These "fax modems" cost only a few dollars more, and we think they're a good deal. A fax modem is a great convenience if you spend much of your time feeding paper through a fax machine at your home or office.

HOW MAGAZINES RATE MODEMS

When magazines review modems, they rate them on three criteria: reliability, interoperability, and throughput. Let's take them one at a time.

➤ **Reliability**   Some modems are prone to failure due to overheating. Make sure you buy a modem that's well ventilated, especially if you plan to leave it on for long periods of time.

➤ **Interoperability**   All modems that follow the standards set by the Consultative

We're also seeing many newer modems with voice mail built in. That means they can act as answering machines—just like your regular phone answering machine, they will let you record outgoing and incoming messages. Of course, to be effective, you'll have to leave your computer on all the time. We think you're probably better off having a separate answering machine unless you need the multiple voice mail boxes these voice/data modems offer to make your home office business sound bigger than it is.

Our general recommendation: Buy the fastest fax/modem you can afford, and leave the other frills for the folks on expense accounts.

Don't buy just any modem: There really are differences between brands. And the best modem isn't always the best known, or the most expensive.

One other thing to note: Internal modems—the ones designed to go inside the computer—are manufactured to work with either PCs or Macs, but not both. External modems will work with any machine as long as you have the right cabling. So if you own a Macintosh, you can buy any external modem that performs well, just make sure to get the appropriate cable.

78. **I just want to send e-mail and visit some bulletin board systems. How fast a modem do I really need?**

—Bare Bones in Baton Rouge

If you're just going to sign on, get your mail and sign off again, you might be able to get by with a relatively slow 2,400 or 9,600 bps modem, but you'll only save a few dollars by buying one of these tortoises.

Committee for International Telephone and Telegraph (CCITT) are supposed to work well together. They don't always. Check the magazine reviews for potential problems before you buy.

➤ **Throughput**   Most people buy modems based on speed. They're certainly priced that way. But not all modems rated at 14,400 bits of data per second are really that fast. Again, here's where the reviews will tell you the truth.

We don't recommend a modem slower than 14.4 kbps. That's the most common modem out there. Newer super high-speed modems that transfer data at twice that rate are starting to be all the rage, but they're so new that most online services still don't support their faster speeds. Remember, you can only go as fast as the person on the other end of the telephone line. It's like buying a car that can hit speeds of 200 miles per hour to drive on an interstate with a speed limit of 55.

But as super high-speed modems become more common, we'll probably see more places that offer high-speed 28.8 kbps connections. So unless you're prepared to buy another modem in a year or two, you might want to consider spending a little extra to get a super high-speed modem.

> *We don't recommend any modem slower than 14.4 kbps. Remember, you can also go as fast as the guy on the other end of the telephone line.*

MODEM STANDARDS: THE NUMBERS GAME

The CCITT sets standards for how modems communicate, and modem makers typically use these Greek-sounding designations to describe their products. Here's what the designations are and what they mean in plain English.

Keep in mind that the V stands for version, followed by a period (pronounced "dot") and the standard number. Look for modems that are "compliant" with these standards, not merely "compatible."

➤ **V.22** 1,200 bps data communications. You won't see any of these modems except in a museum.

➤ **V.22bis** 2,400 bps modem speed. A successor to V.22 (*bis* is Latin for second). The slowest kind you can still buy.

➤ **V.29** The fax standard used by Group III fax machines and fax/modems running at 9,600 bps.

➤ **V.32** 9,600 bps.

➤ **V.32bis** 14,400 bps. Successor to V.32.

➤ **V.32ter** 19,200 bps. Successor to V.32*bis*. (*ter* is Latin for third). This standard was a short-lived interim solution. You should avoid it and go with either V.32*bis* or V.34.

➤ **V.FAST** Non-standard 28,800 bps modems. Avoid these like the plague, they don't work with anything! If you've got one, upgrade it to V.34 as quickly as you can.

79. Should I get an internal modem or an external modem?

—Can't Decide in Canton

We usually tell people to get an external modem. That's a modem that sits outside the computer and is connected via cable to the computer's serial port.

External modems are much easier to install. Putting your new external modem to work involves nothing more than getting the right cable, plugging it in, and turning it on. You won't have to hassle with such arcana as IRQ conflicts, DMA channels, and incorrect i/o addresses. That alone makes it worth it.

Another benefit of buying an external modem is that you can use it with other computers. You just disconnect the cable and take the modem with you. External modems can work with any computer as long as you have the right cabling.

We also like external modems because they're easy to hang up. From time to time during a telecommunciations session you'll find that things get stuck. Your modem crashes and won't release the telephone line. To reset an external modem, though, you just turn it off and on again using its power switch. With an internal modem the only solution is to restart the entire machine.

> ➤ **V.34** 28,800 bps. This standard was just ratified in late 1994. These super-high speed modems should become common in the next few years. They represent the highest speed that can be transmitted over standard voice telephone lines.
> ➤ **V.42** An error-correction standard. Most modern modems have this built in to reduce the number of data errors.
> ➤ **V.42bis** Hardware data-compression. This reduces the size of your data up to four times before transmission, speeding up transmission. A V.*32bis* modem with V.42*bis* data compression can transmit 56,600 bits of data per second—on a good day with the wind at its back. Again, most modern high-speed modems support this standard.
> ➤ **ISDN** Integrated Services Digital Network. The next generation of data communications will use special digital phone lines, instead of regular phone lines. ISDN can move an impressive 128,000 bits per second—that's over 10 times what the older lines can accomplish. To use ISDN, you'll need to install special ISDN phone lines and ante up more money for your monthly bills.

External modems also have lights in front that tell you what's going on. Whoopee! Lots of people love to watch their modems light up when they're going online. And once you know what these lights mean (see question 81), you'll have an easier time figuring out what's wrong with your modem the next time it has problems.

We hope we've convinced you that an external modem is a better buy than an internal one. But, you may ask, why do so many people buy internal modems? There are three reasons.

➤ First, internal modems are cheaper. You don't have to pay extra for the fancy case and lights.

➤ Second, internal modems take up less space because they're inside the computer, not on top of it. And you don't have the messy cabling and power cords to deal with.

➤ Third, high-speed internal modems sometimes work better with Windows. On some older PCs the serial ports aren't fast enough to keep up with high-speed modems. An internal modem doesn't use the serial port so it's not a problem.

We've seen so many people lose sleep over modem configuration problems that we've become firm believers in external modems. Do yourself a favor and keep your modem where it belongs—outside your computer.

External modems are easier to install. They can work with any computer as long as you have the right cabling. They also have cool little lights in front!

80. How does a fax modem work? Where do I put in the paper?

—Faxing in Fairfax

Oh, come on. You're kidding, right? That's the one thing fax modems can't do—fax paper documents. But in all other respects, fax modems are great products that we heartily recommend.

A data modem that also has the ability to send and receive faxes won't cost much more, and you'll find that faxing adds a lot of value. Even if you don't do much faxing now, you'll love having the ability to quickly send out a fax instead of a letter or e-mail. It's also nice to be able to receive faxes from time to time.

When you buy a fax modem, you'll get fax software, too. These programs all work the same way. They tell your computer to think of the fax modem as if it were a printer. (Come to think of it, faxing is no different from printing on a remote printer.) To send the fax you change your computer's "default" printer to the fax modem, then instruct your application to print. The fax software will ask you for information for your fax cover sheet, including a fax number to dial, then it will send the fax.

Computer-generated faxes are much crisper and easier to read, and they save lots of paper. Instead of having to print your document on paper and then feed it through the fax machine, you'll send it directly over the phone line.

Of course, that's also the drawback. If you want to fax something that's already on paper, you won't be able to. That's one reason why a fax modem isn't a perfect replacement for a stand-alone fax machine. Another drawback is that in order to receive faxes, you'll have to leave your computer on all the time. What a waste of energy! Some new computer models, like IBM's Aptiva line, will turn themselves on when the phone rings, receive the fax, and turn themselves off. That saves energy, but it means you have to have a dedicated fax phone line. You wouldn't want to have your computer turn itself on every time Aunt Martha called to talk about the weather.

81. My modem looks like a UFO! What are those weird sounds coming out of it? And what are the flashing lights all about?

—Seeing Things in Seacliff

It's nothing to worry about. Your modem is acting perfectly normal. The weird sounds are just the noises the modem makes while it's connecting with another modem. And the flashing lights are there to tell you what's going on during your telecommunications session. Let's explain what's behind the noise and lights.

Both the noises and the lights are used to monitor the progress of your connection. If you find the noise annoying, you can tell your modem to be silent. And if the lights are distracting, you can always face the modem toward the wall. But for now, let's talk about how a modem works.

First the noises. As we already told you, your modem works by converting data into sound that can be transported over voice lines. By default, most modems leave their speakers on until the connection is made so you know what's happening.

When you begin your online session, the first thing the modem will do is pick up the phone line. You should hear a second or two of dial tone, followed by the sound of the modem dialing. Just like a regular phone call, the phone on the other end will ring until the modem on the other end picks up.

By listening to these sounds, you've verified that your modem can communicate with your software, is connecting properly to the telephone line, and can dial out. You also know if there's a modem or a human at the other end. And this is one of the most important reasons to listen to your modem as it connects.

There's nothing more annoying than getting a dozen late night calls from a computer that thinks your number is an online system.

The first time you dial any number with your modem, you should listen to make sure there's a computer at the other end. You'll know by the high-pitched squealing. (That's opposed, of course, to the shrill profanity you'll hear when you accidentally call a human with your computer.) If you do get a human, pick up the phone, apologize politely, and check the number you're dialing. Or you can do as we do and hang up quickly before they figure out it's you.

When the modem on the other end answers there's a brief period of caterwauling known as "handshaking" or "negotiation." The conversation goes something like this:

"Hi, I'm a modem. Are you?"

"You bet. What speed do you want to talk at?"

"I can do 14.4 kbps. Can you?"

"Sure can. Let's try it."

"Oh, that's fast. Can you read me at this speed or are we getting so many errors that we should slow down?"

"I read you loud and clear. Let's go!"

This conversation is accomplished by squeals, wails, and whines of varying pitches. If all goes well, your modem will signal you with the message "Connect" on your screen, followed by the speed at which you've connected, and information about any error correction or compression it's using. It should also shut off the speaker so that you can proceed with your online session in tranquil silence. Some software won't show you the connect messages, but if you're online, rest assured the modem sent them.

Now, if you can't connect, the modem will hang up and return an error message. Typical error messages include "No Dial Tone," "No Carrier" (that means it wasn't able to reach another modem), "No Answer," and "Voice."

If you really want to turn off those hideous squealing sounds you can issue a silence command to your modem before you dial. This command varies but is usually ATM0. (Note that the "0" here is a zero, not the letter O.) Check your modem documentation to make sure. Your software may also have a switch to turn off the modem's speaker. And most external modems with speakers also have a volume control.

That's the sound. Now for the lights. We're going to describe a typical set of modem lights. Yours may vary. Some modems have character readouts instead. And a few modems have no indicators at all. We prefer modems that tell you what they're up to.

Take a look at the illustration . Here's what each of those lights means and what they do. You may have additional lights, but this is the basic set.

Your basic external modem

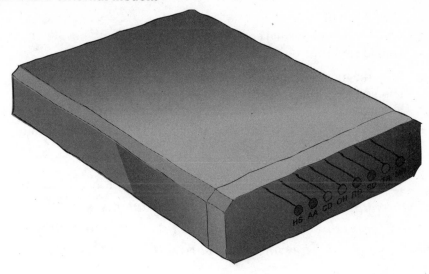

➤ **HS = High Speed**   Lights up when you're communicating at 9,600 bps or better.

➤ **AA = Auto Answer**   Lights up when your modem is in auto answer mode. When in AA mode, the modem will answer the phone if it rings.

➤ **CD = Carrier Detect**   Lights up when you're online with another modem. (The other modem's signal is called its "carrier.")

➤ **OH = Off Hook**   Lights up when your modem has picked up the phone. If your modem is off the hook it's the same as if your phone were off the hook. No incoming calls will be accepted.

➤ **RD = Receive Data**   Lights up whenever data is received from the remote system.

➤ **SD = Send Data**   Lights up whenever your system is sending data.

➤ **TR = Terminal Ready**   Lights up when you run your telecommunications software. It's a signal to the modem that you're ready to rock 'n' roll.

➤ **MR = Modem Ready**   Lights up when your modem is ready to use. Should be lit whenever your modem is on.

Q/A

The normal sequence of lights is as follows:

1. When you turn your modem on, the MR light should light up and stay lit.

2. When you start your telecommunications software, the TR light should go on, too.

3. When you send the dial command to your modem, the OH light should come on.

4. After the modem connects with the remote system, the CD light should be on, and if you're communicating at high speed, the HS light should be on.

5. During your session, the SD and RD lights should flicker back and forth as you send and receive data.

If you really want to turn off those hideous squealing sounds you can issue a silence command to your modem before you dial. The command varies, but you can usually just type ATM0.

If the lights do something different, it will give you some idea of what's going wrong. For example, if you see SD on, but never see RD, it means you're sending but not receiving data. Maybe the system on the other end is down.

If you don't get the TR light, your cabling might be incorrect or damaged. If MR doesn't light, there's something internally wrong with your modem. And so on.

There's no way to disable the modem lights, but if they really bug you, turn the modem toward the wall, or stick some electrical tape over the front panel.

82. My modem didn't come with any cables. What do I need?

—Disconnected in Deland

There's nothing more disappointing than getting home with your new toy only to find you'll have to make another trip to the store before you can use it. If you have an external modem, the cable is necessary to connect your modem to your computer's serial port. Don't leave the store without it.

You can take comfort in the fact that modems are pretty generic. There's no such thing as a Mac modem or a PC modem. The only difference is in the cabling. Some modem packages, particularly on the Mac side, come with cabling. Check the box again. If you're sure your modem came cable-free, so to speak, go back to the store and get one.

Before you make your shopping trip, check the back of your computer. Note the size and shape and gender of your serial port so that you can buy a matching cable. For instance, are the connectors "male" or "female?" Male connectors have pins that stick out. Female connectors have holes for the pins to fit into. Your cable will have to have the opposite gender connector to mate properly with your serial port. You didn't know computing could be this sexy, did you?

Also, how many fork-like pins are there, or how many holes? All of this is very important. Almost all PC serial ports use male "DB-9" connectors, which is a just a fancy way of saying a rectangular connector with 9-pins. The original Macs also used male DB-9 connectors, but all modern Macs use female 8-pin "DIN" connectors.

Most modems have a female DB-25 connector in back. Some smaller modems save space by using DB-9 connectors. And the really tiny ones may use a proprietary connector that forces you to buy a cable designed for that specific modem.

So the most common PC modem cable has a male DB-25 at the modem end and a female DB-9 at the computer end. Mac modem cables usually come with a male DB-25 at the modem end and a male DIN-9 at the computer end. If you're getting a fast Mac modem, 14.4 kbps or better, make sure to get a specially wired "high-speed modem" cable.

If all else fails, draw a sketch or take a picture of the back of your computer and bring it into the computer store. The service techs will enjoy talking about you for years to come, but who cares?

83. **I'm having trouble getting my modem working. When I called tech support they said I needed to "modify my init string." Huh?**

—Larkspur Lingophobe

"Modify your init string." Now, there's a phrase to strike fear into the heart of any new computer user. Even to many experienced computer users, it's totally unintelligible.

"Init" is short for initialization. The init "string" is a series of numbers and letters you send to your modem to configure it before you dial out. There. Feel any better? Here's a typical init string: AT&F&C1&D2W2 S7=60S11=60%C0.

Makes a lot of sense, doesn't it? All init strings begin with AT, which stands for attention and tells the modem to listen up. The gibberish that follows is the actual configuration information. Don't ask us what it means!

Modem problems, particularly fax problems, can often be traced back to a faulty init string. The problem is, the design of these strings is often a black art. It's certainly not something you'd want to experiment with.

Telecommunications programs generally come preconfigured with init strings for the most popular modems. If you're lucky, your modem is one of them. That's one reason it pays to get a well known modem.

If your telecommunications program doesn't have a configuration setting for your particular modem you can always use the "generic" or "Hayes-compatible" setting. Hayes made the first popular modems, and they set the standard for modem commands. To this day the commands you issue to your modem are very likely based on the original Hayes commands, with some additions for the added capabilities.

All "init strings" begin with AT, which stands for attention and tells the modem to listen up. The gibberish that follows is the actual configuration information. Don't ask us what it means!

If you still can't get your modem working, there are several places to go for help. Call tech support for both the modem manufacturer and the software vendor. They may know something about getting this stuff working that didn't make it into the manual.

You can also pose the question online (if you can get that far). One of the great things about online services like CompuServe, Prodigy, and America Online is that there are lots of people who know a whole lot more about this stuff than any sane person should. And they're usually ready to help out if you ask politely.

84. **Everybody is talking about how hip it is to be online, but where exactly is this place? I mean, when they say "online," exactly what and where are they talking about?**

—Dense in Delaware

"Online" isn't really a place. It's more like an activity: not somewhere you go, but something you use your computer to "do." We've talked about how a modem works. Now it's time to talk about what you can do once you've got it working. And one of the most interesting things you could possibly do with it is go "online."

The easiest way to get online is to subscribe to an "online service." The big three online services, CompuServe, America Online, and Prodigy, boast nearly five million members between them. People call the services, or "log in," to do everything from getting the latest news and sports information right off the wire to forming discussion groups. They get online to do a little shopping, play games with each other, and send mail (known as electronic mail, or e-mail) to other subscribers. So even though online isn't a real place, for the millions of people who gather online there is a real sense of place. They may be alone sitting in front of their computer, but in a very real way, they're getting together with friends to have a good time.

Online services run on huge computers based in a central location. For example, America Online is in Vienna, Virginia. CompuServe is in Columbus, Ohio. But it doesn't matter where the actual computers are located. To keep your long distance costs down, the online services provide local phone numbers for most areas. These computers can handle tens of thousands of calls at the same time. Every night they become a meeting place for people from all over the country.

So which online service is best for you? That depends. The services overlap quite a bit in the kinds of things they offer, but each service cultivates its own personality. To find the right service, you'll have to find one that matches your style.

The granddaddy of services, H&R Block's CompuServe, is not only the largest, but it also offers the widest variety of information. It's full of great business resources like stock quotes, financial news, and technical discussion groups (called Forums) where you can ask hardware and software whizzes for help. It's certainly a best bet for businesses and anyone who needs to do research.

Prodigy, a joint venture of IBM and Sears, is aimed at families, and has an excellent choice of activities for kids as well as Mom and Dad. America Online (AOL) is another great family system, and currently is the fastest growing online service. It is an especially good place for online discussions. AOL's Chat Rooms are humming every night and well into the wee hours of the morning. It also happens to sport one of the most attractive and easy-to-use interfaces.

Then there's the rest of the pack. Services like General Electric's GEnie, AT&T's The Imagination Network, Apple's eWorld, Dow Jones, and Rupert Murdoch's Delphi Internet all have their charms. And Microsoft Corporation is about to join the group with the Microsoft Network (MSN). Since its software will be bundled with every copy of Windows 95, we expect that MSN will grow very quickly. And of course, there's the Internet. We'll talk more about that later.

There's nothing that says you can't join more than one of these services. But the costs do add up. Most services charge a monthly fee of around $10. For that you'll get four or five hours per month online. You'll find that those free hours fly by pretty quickly, and then the meter starts running. All these services charge at least $2.50 per hour for the time you're dialed into them. Some charge much more. And many of the services charge a premium for some of their features. If cost is an issue, Prodigy and America Online offer the best deals, but you can still expect to pay more than $25 per month for even moderate use.

So shop around. Your modem probably came with introductory accounts on several of the services. Take the plunge. Sign up for a few of them, tour around, and see if you can find a good fit. You might discover a whole new world, without ever leaving your computer.

Q/A

85. What is a BBS? How is it different from an online service?

—*Bumbling in Beaverton*

The big online services notwithstanding, the bulk of online activity happens on "bulletin board systems," or BBSs. These systems are usually local, run for fun by people who call themselves Sysops, short for system operators. Anybody can be a Sysop. All you need to do is install a phone line, set up a computer, stick some information people might want on it, then publish the number so the world can dial in.

> *The bulk of online activity happens on bulletin board systems. We can tell you for a fact that there's a BBS somewhere, someplace, for every possible interest under the sun.*

At last count, there were over 50,000 BBSs in the U.S. There's a BBS somewhere someplace for virtually every interest under the sun. For instance, our local jazz station has a BBS that listeners can dial into to post requests, review new jazz albums, even find out about local jazz performances. There are BBSs that cater specifically to the needs of Windows users, Mac users, even baseball card collectors and gourmet cooks.

It may take a little effort to get that first BBS number. Check with a local computer user group, or look in the back of computer magazines. *Computer Shopper* magazine publishes a BBS list every month, arranged by area code. But once you get on that first BBS you'll almost always find a list of other boards you can call. And from there, the online world is your oyster.

Many BBSs charge their users, but the fee is generally much lower than online services, usually no more than $5 per month. Of course, there's not nearly the depth of information and activities on BBSs that there is on the big online services. And BBSs most often have only one or two lines, so busy signals are common. But, for more than a few of us, the local BBS has taken the place of the grange hall, the cracker barrel, or the coffee shop as a place to meet, greet, and swap tall tales.

86. What kind of software do I need to get online?

—*Terminally Challenged in Topeka*

Everyone needs special software to get online. That software is typically called "telecommunications" software, or "telecom," or "com" software for short. You probably got some with your modem.

The limited edition versions that come with most modems don't have all the bells and whistles that their big brothers have, though. If you spend a lot of time online, you'll probably want to upgrade to the full-fledged versions of these packages. You'll also see dozens of telecom programs at your local computer software store. And once you get online, you'll find a wide choice of free or inexpensive software, too. There's no hurry to buy a big expensive telecom program. Get your feet wet online first, and you'll get a better idea of what you really need.

The simplest kind of telecom software just turns your smart computer into a dumb terminal. You know, like the ones they use to check your seat assignments at the airport. These programs are called "terminal emulators." Windows comes with one, it's called Terminal. Good name. You use terminal emulators to set the modem speed and communications settings, dial the remote computer, and get online. From that point on, most of the work is being done by the remote computer and echoed onto your local screen by the terminal software.

Don't make the mistake of confusing an online service with a telecom package. The software is just what you use to access the online service. It's like a window into the remote computer. Some online services, like America Online and Prodigy, have their own specialized telecom software that makes them much easier to use. When you sign up for these services you'll get a copy of the software.

If you're going to wade into that ocean called the Internet, you'll need additional specialized communications software. Check out question 94 for more information.

87. How do I keep my online bills reasonable?

—Pinching Pennies in Pasadena

Hah! Good luck. Online bills have a way of sneaking up on you. With your cable bill you always know how much you're going to pay. You may hate paying it, but at least there are no surprises.

When you're online, though, time is money—lots of it. Here are some ways to keep your online bill from going through the roof.

➤ **Keep track of how much time you've spent online.** Most of the services give you four or five free hours every month. Make sure you know when you've used up that free time. Knowing that the clock is ticking has a wonderful way of keeping you on task. Most every telecom program has some way of showing you how long you've been online.

➤ **Do what you can off-line.** Prepare your e-mail before you log in, then mail it and get off. CompuServe, America Online, and Prodigy all offer a way to dial in, quickly gather all your mail, then sign off so you can read and answer it when the clock's not running. It doesn't make sense to spend three bucks an hour to fine-tune your purple prose!

➤ **Use the systems when others aren't.** All the big online services slow down when lots of users are logged on, and a slow response time means you'll spend a lot of time waiting for the remote computer. The busiest times are from 7 p.m. to 1 a.m. Eastern time. We try to log on during the day to avoid the log jams. But beware, some systems charge more during business hours. Read your service agreement and stick with the cheaper times.

➤ **Look for a flat fee service.** Flat fee services charge you one monthly fee, no matter how much time you spend online. Kind of like your cable company. None of the big three offer flat fee rates, but many Internet connections work this way. And so do most BBSs.

➤ **And don't forget your phone bill.** Remember that you have to call these services over the telephone line. If you aren't calling a local number, the long distance charges will add up a lot faster than the online charges. Stick with services that have local or toll-free telephone numbers.

None of these tips will help one bit once your teenagers discover that they can gab with other kids online. But at least you can do your part to keep from going to the poorhouse.

88. Is it okay for my kids to go online?

—Parental in Pacifica

Who's going to stop them? It's no wonder the fastest growing audience for online services these days is the under-18 set. This is the first truly high-tech generation, after all, and they're more at home in cyberspace than we'll ever be.

The online world is absolutely intoxicating, especially for kids too young to drive or date. Many kids even report a certain amount of peer pressure to log on. Kids love to join chats and discussions online, where no one can tell how old they are or what clique they're in at school. Even more interesting, online adults treat them as equals. Think of how incredibly empowering this is for a kid.

Used wisely, online resources can be terrifically educational. Grade schoolers will find the online homework helpers on America Online and Prodigy to be just the ticket to help with a tough math or writing assignment. And because it is so easy to search for news and articles online, kids can use online services to make detailed book reports and current events projects. Instead of just writing a report on life during World War II, a resourceful kid can dial up the SeniorNet section of America Online and chat with some people who could tell her what it was like firsthand.

But bear in mind: Even though kids are extraordinarily sophisticated in all matters technical—and even though there are fantastic resources for their education and entertainment there—there's some pretty steamy stuff going on, too.

Q/A

There are whole areas dedicated to nothing but sexy pictures. And even the "family" online services have their share of perverts prowling the virtual corridors. It's not like anyone is checking IDs at the door.

So keep an eye on your kids when they're online, and teach them safe online behavior. Rule One: You don't know who you're chatting with, so never give out your address or phone number, or heaven forbid, your password. Rule Two: If anyone says anything that scares you or sounds weird, tell Mom or Dad immediately. And, parents, if you spot a weirdo, report them to the online service.

> *Even though kids will find some extraordinary resources for education and entertainment online, you should know there's some pretty steamy stuff going on there, too.*

Life online is no different from life in any public place. For the most part it's a wonderful resource for kids. Just don't assume that because they're "safe" at home when they're online, they don't need to be supervised.

89. What can I do online?

—Excited in Exeter

You can do everything you can do in the real world, but with a bizarre twist. You'll never have to leave your chair to do any of it. That should do wonders for your waistline.

By subscribing to an online service, you'll have access to a whole world of activities: You can send e-mail to anyone else that's online, you can shop for anything and everything (including groceries), you can download up-to-the-minute news, banking info, stock quotes, financial information, and even lottery numbers. You can get lots of free software—not to mention free advice and conversation on virtually every topic you can imagine, from astrology to zoology.

You can also attend live "conferences" and "concerts," where celebrities appear online to answer questions from their fans. Many news shows on TV and on the radio now have live online discussion groups going on as they air. That means you can send your comments, questions, and answers to the hosts and guests while they're on the air.

90. **How can I meet people online?**

—Looking for Love in L.A.

The real question is, how can you help "not" meeting people online? Online socializing is just a part of online life. It's a huge part, in fact. Very few of the people who go online do so just to anonymously download software or information, or to just lurk invisibly behind the scenes in discussion groups. And if they do, they don't for long.

There is something incredibly enticing about meeting people online for the first time. Because the people you meet aren't distracted by appearances, you can really get to know each other there. Sure, there are countless stories of people meeting online and later marrying, but even relationships of the platonic variety can be enormously appealing online. You'll find that you're running into the same people in the same discussion groups or online again and again, and after a while you'll have a whole new set of online acquaintances and friends. And you don't even have to ever meet them in person, unless you want to.

You can really get to know each other "before" committing to a first meeting in person. There are countless stories of people meeting online and later marrying.

Do approach your new online social life with caution, though. Be aware that the veil of anonymity allowed by an online service sometimes tempts people into taking on an entire new identity. Women you meet may be actually men, and the other way around. One famous online "love" story from a few years back is of two people—a 33-year-old woman and 35-year-old man—who met and fell in love online. They spent hours online getting to know each other before they agreed to finally meet. And as it turned it out, the couple—instead of being a man and woman in their 30s—was a boy in his teens and a 72-year-old man. Wow. We hear they're still friends, though.

Finally, be careful about divulging too much personal information to online friends and contacts. It's rare, but there is such a thing as "online stalking." Be careful with personal details such as your address of your home or work, credit details, and the like. And never—we can't stress this enough—give out your credit card number or e-mail password to someone who asks. There is no reason for it, no matter what they say.

91. How can I get free software online?

—Broke in Brookfield

One of the best reasons to get a modem and go online is to score free software. You do that by "downloading" it from a remote computer. We're not talking about pirating commercial software. We're talking about software that's been put online specifically for you to download and use. The big online services have literally tens of thousands of utilities, games, graphics, sounds, and videos for you to download. Even small BBSs may have hundreds of files to chose from.

There are three kinds of files you'll find online: freeware, shareware, and demos. Freeware is software that is being given away by its author. Freeware programs are usually small utilities, but on occasion you'll find a freeware program that rivals the commercial offerings for functionality. The best Macintosh antivirus program, for example, Disinfectant, is given away by its altruistic author John Norstad. John and a team of volunteers keep the software up to date, and make it available almost everywhere.

> *One of the best reasons to get a modem and go online is that you can score lots of software for free. The big online services have literally tens of thousands of games, graphics, sounds, videos, and computer maintenance utilities you can download and use.*

Shareware software is also freely available online, but the author asks you to send him or her money if you end up using it. There's a lot of very good shareware out there. In fact, that's how the best-selling game of 1994, Doom, started out. It's estimated that there are over 10 million copies of the shareware version of Doom in circulation. If you find yourself using a shareware program regularly, we encourage you to send in the shareware fee. It'll give its author some incentive to keep it up to date, and give other programmers a reason to consider this grassroots form of distribution.

More and more big software companies are putting demo versions of their commercial programs online, too. These programs are usually disabled in some way. They can't be printed, or can only work with a few files at a time. But it's a good way to try before you buy.

All telecom software has the ability to download files—that's one of the most popular things to do online. Your manual should tell you how to begin.

92. How do I keep from looking stupid online?

—*Shy in Chicago*

Too late. If you even have to ask, chances are you're already doing something somebody out there thinks is stupid. But who cares what they think? This isn't a popularity contest, you know. One of the things we dislike most about online life is the snotty netsurfers who like nothing better than to intimidate newcomers like yourself. The heck with them. Fortunately, as loud and obnoxious as they are, they're a very small minority. Most people online are just nice people who are looking for new people to meet and places to explore.

It's always good to observe some common courtesy when you do go online. Before joining a new discussion group look around for a Frequently Asked Questions (FAQ) file. That's where the ground rules and guidelines for that particular group will be posted. It's also where you can quietly get the general answers you need without bugging someone else for them. Entering a new group is just like joining an ongoing party. It helps to know what the customs are before you open your mouth.

WHEN IN ROME...

There are a few things you should know about all online interactions.
➤ **Don't type in ALL UPPERCASE LETTERS. It looks like you're shouting and is considered quite rude.**
➤ **Keep your messages brief and to the point, and try to put them where they belong. No one wants to spend time wading through irrelevant or confusing communciations.**
➤ **If you're responding to someone else's message, it's polite to repeat the relevant parts of the earlier message. For example, it's much better to write:**

```
To: Jerry
From: Leo
RE: Birthday Cakes
On March 9, 1995 Jerry wrote:
> Whoever thought of putting carrots in cakes
> must have been nuts.
I agree!
```

than to just send a message saying "I agree." By convention, the portions preceded by the angle brackets (>) are quoted from the previous message. It gives everyone reading your message, including the original author, some context for your comments.

Q/A

93. I hear a lot about the Internet these days, but what is it?

—Confused in Colorado

It kills us. You can't pick up the paper anymore without hearing some sort of reference to the Internet, but they never, ever say what they mean by it. In fact, many give the impression that the Internet is just something you can buy, or something you can subscribe to, along the lines of a CompuServe or America Online. But it isn't.

The Internet is a network of computer networks. Now, don't you feel better? You see, back when the Cold War was still in full swing, the government decided it would be a good idea to have a computer system that could survive a nuclear attack. So it funded something called the Advanced Research Projects Agency, which came up with ARPANet, the granddaddy of the Internet. ARPANet was designed to have no central location, that is, nowhere to target during a nuclear war. And even if some of its computers were lost, the network could continue running. ARPANet has grown by leaps and bounds into the so-called Internet we know today.

The Internet is a network of computer networks. Now, don't you feel better?

The Internet is a worldwide phenomenon now. It even extends into Russia and China. But there's still no central authority. In fact, ARPA doesn't even exist any more. Today there are three million computer networks connected to the Internet. Moreover, communication over the net is completely distributed. A message you send from New York to Washington, D.C. might travel thousands of miles through a dozen systems before reaching its destination.

Each system on the Internet volunteers some of its system resources for Internet users. That can mean something as simple as agreeing to pass mail along, to something as awesome as offering gigabytes of data free for the downloading. The Internet is the only working anarchy we know of, and it works because everybody on the net generously donates to the net.

Some of the things you'll find on the net include the Usenet Newsgroups, over 12,000 public special interest discussion groups that cover topics as wide ranging as football, sex, and Barney the dinosaur. You'll also find files for downloading gigabytes of data from all over the world. And, of course, the Internet acts as a global e-mail service. Every Internet user has a unique e-mail address. All 30 million of them.

The Internet is much larger than any online service—much larger than all of them put together, in fact, since they're all part of the net. This year all three big online services, CompuServe, America Online, and Prodigy, will offer unrestricted access to the Internet. You can already use them to read NewsGroups and send mail. In the months to come you'll also be able to download files using the Internet's File Transfer Protocol (FTP), and, most importantly, you'll be able to do the one thing that has single-handedly led to an explosion of interest in the Internet: "browse the Web."

We bet you've heard of the Web: It's short for the "World Wide Web," or WWW. It was created by particle physicists at the CERN Research lab in Geneva as a way to publish their papers online. But it's become much more than that—the Web now gives you point-and-click access to the net, along with stunning full color graphics. You can browse hundreds or thousands of files and locations, just by clicking on a "hotword." Say you were reading an article about Jimmy Carter. If the word "peanuts" in that article were "hot," you could click on it to display all kinds of articles about peanuts. The peanut article might have a reference to Georgia State University, which you could in turn click on to read about the school. The Web really is a web of vast and interlocking pieces of information.

To navigate the Web you use special software called a "Web browser." You'll find many different Web browsers online, but the most popular are Mosaic and Netscape. Until the appearance of the Web, you had to be conversant with an operating system called UNIX to get around. Now even computer novices can interact with the Internet like old pros.

There, we've done it. We've told you all about the Internet without once using that overworked phrase "information superhighway." Suffice it to say, the only real information superhighway is the Internet, and it's here right now, just waiting for you to hitch a ride.

94. How do I get on the Internet?

—Eager in Evanston

It's the $64,000 question. And there's no easy answer. The one thing holding back the Internet (if you can use such an expression about something that's growing at the rate of 10 percent a month) is that it's not so easy to get on to it. Fact is, it can be pretty tough.

Most of the people on the net get a connection through their schools or workplaces. That's why there's a preponderance of college kids and researchers on the Internet.

If you're not lucky enough to have a courtesy connection, you'll have to buy an account with a company that serves as an "Internet Service Provider" (ISP). Think of your ISP as your on-ramp to the information superhighway (if you'll pardon this over-used metaphor).

Your local ISP sets up a computer network that it hooks right into the Internet's network of networks. Then, for a fee, your ISP will let you dial into its network, and from there onto the Internet.

The fee varies, depending on the kind of service you want and the ISP itself. The cheapest kind of Internet account is something called a Personal Shell. For around $17.50 per month you'll be able to dial into their system using a simple terminal program to access the Internet. But then you'll be stuck using UNIX commands and text-based interfaces like Gopher and Lynx. You won't be able to browse the Web in full color.

To do that you need a "SLIP" or "PPP" account. These accounts network your computer directly onto the Internet through your ISP's connection. You become one with the 3 million other Internet computers.

Once you're actually on the network, you can run more sophisticated software on your own machine. Programs like Netscape, Mosaic, and Eudora are easier to use, and much prettier than their text-based UNIX counterparts. Prices for these networked accounts have been dropping fast. They're now almost as cheap as the old fashioned Personal Shell accounts. We're seeing prices of around $20 per month, with hourly connect charges of a dollar or two.

But be warned: Not only are those prices comparable to the charges you'll get from a big online service, but your bill may mount even faster since there's so much more stuff on the Internet. Watch out that you don't rack up too much time and money out there in cyberspace.

Be warned: Not only is surfing the Internet just as expensive as joining an online service, sometimes it's even more expensive. There's a lot of stuff to take up your time there!

And speaking of online services, they're moving into the ISP business, too. As we mentioned in the previous answer, CompuServe, America Online, and Prodigy will offer full Internet connections this year. And the new Microsoft Network, scheduled to debut in August 1995, will also offer access to the net. Odds are good that within a year or so, the simplest way to get on the Internet will be to subscribe to a big online service.

95.

What kinds of things are on the Internet? Can it take the place of an online service? And how can I find out where things are?

—*North Dakota Newbie*

The first time you get on the Internet you might get a touch of vertigo. There's so much stuff, so many people, it's all so overwhelming! It may be the only time you'll ever get a sense of just how incredibly huge the world really is.

For this reason, finding particular things on the Internet is difficult. It's like an overstuffed closet. You know what you want is in there, but how can you get to it? Remember that this is a disorganized anarchy, there's no central authority keeping track of everything. Yes, there are several search tools that have been designed to overcome this inherent chaos, including programs named Archie and Veronica, and people have made various attempts to organize everything. But things change so fast on the net that no organizational system can last long. It's really best not to think of the Internet as a research tool. Not, at least, until you've spent some time there learning about its organizational quirks. The online services are really much better for finding the things you need.

On the other hand, the Internet is great if you're the type that likes to browse information with no goal in particular. The less goal-oriented you are, the more you'll like the net. The best way to deal with the Internet is to find a little corner of it that you can call home. Then as you get used to all the hubbub, slowly venture out and expand your horizons.

For many people that first stop on the net is the Usenet NewsGroups. As we've mentioned, there are more than 12,000 groups discussing all kinds of topics. But the groups are named in such a way that you can select the ones you're interested in. All the computer-oriented groups have names that begin with COMP.

COMP.SYS.MAC, for instance, is where you'll find people who are exchanging public messages about Apple computers. Groups that focus on leisure time activities begin with ALT.DREAMS is a dreams discussion group. There are further divisions. ALT.ANIMALS has groups on badgers (ALT.ANIMALS.BADGERS), bears, (ALT.ANIMALS.BEARS) and lampreys (ALT.ANIMALS.LAMPREYS), among others. The ALT.FAN groups are fan clubs for all kinds of celebrities, including Hello Kitty, David Letterman, and even Power Rangers. There are also regional groupings, national groupings, and more. Most people use specialized news reader software to help make sense of all this.

You may also find a home in a chat area. These are live conversation groups with dozens, even hundreds of people all typing away at the same time. Many people spend hours in their groups every evening. On the Internet you'll use a program called IRC, short for Internet Relay Chat, to join in.

And if you can browse the Web (see question 94) you may find a Web Page that provides a comfortable starting point for your explorations. Web page addresses are called URLs, short for Uniform Resource Locaters (remember computer geeks thought all this up).

For example, Leo's home page URL is http://www.ccnet.com/laporte/. The http stands for HyperText Transfer Protocol, that's the set of conventions that tells the computer how to display these pages.

www.ccnet.com is the address for the Web server Leo's page resides on, and the /laporte/ tells your browser where to look once it gets there. When you tell Mosaic to go to that address, it will contact the server and ask for the information. Once the info gets to your computer, Mosaic will put it up on the screen, and you'll get a picture of Leo as well as some other things, including pointers to other fun pages. Gina's Web page can be found by going to the Ziff-Davis home page at http://www.Ziff.com/.

At last count there were over 30,000 distinct Web pages on the net, covering the entire range of human endeavor, from quantum mechanics to nude volleyball. Most Web pages include at least a few pointers, or links, to other pages, so you can spend hours just clicking from page to page.

Maybe the net is not for you. On the other hand, maybe you'll agree with the millions of new netsurfers who think it is the most exciting new medium since television. And a whole lot more fun.

96. My mom just got a computer too, and both of us have modems. How can we send e-mail to each other?

—Sonny in Springfield

How sweet. You get to regularly correspond with your mom, and you spare your spouse the stress of constant contact with the in-laws to boot? Boy, we applaud this. We really do.

> *The biggest benefit of corresponding with family and friends over e-mail? It's cheaper.*

But there's a second benefit to corresponding with family members and friends over e-mail—it's cheaper. A lot cheaper. Long distance calls add up, and with postal rates going up, the U.S. mail is not much of a bargain anymore. But you can easily find an e-mail service that will let you type private messages to each other any time you feel like it. There are even online services that will let you chat "live" with that special someone. In live online chats, you can type messages and respond to each other almost instantaneously.

To send e-mail you'll both need mailboxes. The easiest way to get a mailbox is to subscribe to a commercial online service such as Ameirca Online or Compu-Serve. They make it easy for people to exchange private e-mail at affordable rates. You don't need to subscribe to the same service, either. Most online services let you e-mail people on other services via the Internet.

The messages you send over an online service are a lot like regular mail—you compose and mail it at a time that's convenient for you, and your mother can read and respond whenever she feels like it, too. And because e-mail is so fast, she can read it just minutes after you send it.

But many online services also offer "chat" rooms, where the sending of messages is a lot more analogous to what goes on in CB radio. It's live—with both of you (and maybe a dozen or so of your closest online friends) typing and responding to each other at more or less the same time.

97. I want to find my old college sweetheart. I bet she's online somewhere, but how do I get her e-mail address?

—Fratboy in Fresno

Time to don your Sam Spade trench coat and fedora and get ready for some detective work!

There is no one way to find someone online. There are just too many services, and there's no central directory. But often, with a little digging, you can e-mail your way to a long-lost friend. You might try some of the following techniques.

First, search the online services you already belong to. Prodigy, CompuServe, America Online, and the rest all have searchable member directories. You won't be able to search the services you aren't a member of. But you could ask a friend to do it.

FOR PROS ONLY

If you're an Internet pro, or you know someone who is, you can use "gopher" to search the various Internet directories. Gopher is a Unix program available on all Internet sites that provides menu-based access to Internet resources. Sit down at the terminal and type GOPHER YALEINFO.YALE.EDU. You'll get the menu for Yale University's gopher site. Select the menu item "Browse YaleInfo (Yale and Internet Information)." Then select "People on the Internet." You'll see a long list of user directories that you can search. If your sweetheart is on the Internet, she'll be in there somewhere.

If you can't find your sweetheart there, it's time to face the big *megillah*—the Internet. There are tens of millions of people all over the world with Internet e-mail addresses. That would be a pretty big phone book, if it even existed. The Internet is so decentralized, though, that you'll have to search in several places to find her.

The first thing to do is see if she's ever posted a message in the "Usenet News-groups." Usenet is the sort of blanket name for the various "news and discussion groups" on the Internet, places where people of common interests meet online to post messages, news, comments, even trade insults. Because so many people post there, there's a chance that your missing sweetheart might be one of them. At least it's worth a try. You can do this by e-mail. Send a message to mail-server@rtfm.mit.edu. (Check with your online service to find out how to send mail to the Internet.) In the body of the message just put one line: send usenet-addresses/ and the name of the person you're looking for.

Now, if she hasn't posted to a Usenet Newsgroup, you'll have to dig a little deeper. Even though there's no complete Internet phone book, there are a num-ber of places you can search. You will need to be able to access the Internet directly to do it, though. If you don't have an Internet account, your local public or university library may. Head on over to their terminal and try the technique in the sidebar.

98. I'm on America Online, but I have friends who are always telling me to send them e-mail on the online services they use. How do I send a message to my friends on Prodigy and MCI Mail without leaving America Online?

—Alone in Altoona

Once you understand some basic addressing rules, it's easy to send messages from one service to another using the Internet. It's all in the address. First, find out what your friend's local address is. Then you'll need the online service's Inter-net address. Finally, combine the two with an @ sign and you've got the full Inter-net address.

For example, if your friend is JoeS on America Online, his Internet address is joes@aol.com.

You get that by combining Joe's local address on America Online, JoeS, with America Online's official Internet address aol.com using the @ sign. Capitaliza-tion is irrelevant. Joe's address is pronounced "joe s at a-o-l dot com." Grizzled Internet veterans always call periods "dots." If Joe has spaces in his name, remove them.

Let's try some more. If your friend is 72241,547 on CompuServe, his Internet address is 72241.547@compuserve.com. Notice that we replace the comma with a period. That's because commas aren't allowed in Internet addresses.

If your friend is G88S88 on Prodigy, her Internet id would be g88s88@prod-igy.com. The MCI Mail address, 480-7500, becomes 4807500@mcimail.com, and so on.

You'll need to check with your online service about how they want you to send mail on the Internet. CompuServe, for example, wants you to add the word INTERNET: to the beginning of an Internet address. America Online, on the other hand, takes the Internet address as is.

Now here's one last trick for those of you who've had the patience to sit through all the "ats," "dots," and "coms." The easiest way to get someone's Inter-net address is to ask them to send *you* mail. When their e-mail comes in, copy the contents of the From: field into your address book. You'll never have to watch your dots and coms again!

TIP

You'll notice that most online services have ".com" in their addresses. That's because com is the traditional Internet extension for commercial systems. Other common abbreviations include .edu for educational institutions, .net or .org for Internet organizations, and .gov for govern-ment systems.

---

99. What do all those funny symbols and abbreviations mean in the e-mail I get? What's the key to the code here?

—Clearwater Cracker

The key here is experience. These online geeks have spent years practicing the fine art of coming up with the crazy acronyms and symbols they use in their e-mail messages and in the chat rooms. It helps them type faster.

For instance, BTW means "by the way." IMHO means "in my humble opin-ion," and RO means "right on!" Well, actually, we just made that last one up, but only to prove a point: People make these little acronyms up all the time, and you'll drive yourself crazy trying to keep up with them.

Plus, don't you think it's a little rude to speak in code in front of strangers? If you feel as if you really must use hip online symbols and conventions in your e-mail, we recommend you gently sprinkle them into your online conversation. Don't overdo it, or you'll look like a jerk.

One of the problems with e-mail is that you can't hear someone's tone of voice or see their facial expressions. So e-mailed comments are sometimes misunderstood because the recipient couldn't tell the author was smiling when she wrote it. To avoid confusion, e-mail experts add cute little smiley icons at the end of their witticisms. It's the e-mail equivalent of a laugh track. The smileys started with the simple :-) (turn your head sideways to see the face), but they've evolved into a whole lexicon, everything from a wink ;-) to a frown :-(to Abe Lincoln =|:-). Oh, puh-leeze.

OK, even though we don't suggest you use them unless under extreme duress (ED), here are some of the more common online abbreviations (COA) and what they mean (WTM).

Common Online Abbreviations	
<g>	Grin
BFN	Bye for now
BRB	Be right back
BTW	By the way
FWIW	For what it's worth
IMHO	In my humble opinion
LOL	Laughing out loud
ROTFL	Rolling on the floor laughing
RSN	Real soon now
RTFM	Read the friggin' manual
TTFN	Ta ta for now

These acronyms change regularly in order to keep new people in the dark. If you see one you don't know, ask the author! He will be secretly thrilled to know that there's someone online who knows even less than he does.

Q/A

100. Is it possible to send my congressional representatives e-mail messages?

—Political in Paducah

What do you want to go and bother them for? They're busy enough whooping it up in Washington.

Seriously, one of the great things about e-mail is that it flattens hierarchies. CEOs read their own e-mail. Movie stars read their own e-mail. Everybody except politicians reads their own e-mail. We know some pols who don't even want their fax numbers to get out because they're afraid of being swamped by faxes from their constituents.

These days, you can easily send e-mail to your local congressmen, or even Mr. President.

Well, heck, we think it's a good idea to write to your representatives in Washington anyway. The best way to get their e-mail addresser is to call the Capitol switchboard at (202) 224-3121.

As of this writing only 40 members of the House of Representatives have e-mail addresses. Each senator is responsible for setting up his or her own e-mail box. As far as we can tell, most of them haven't yet. But as the song says, the times they are a changin', and we bet that in the next few years you'll be able to e-mail anyone you want inside the Beltway.

In the meantime, here are a few important addresses you'll want to add to your little black book.

Bill Clinton	president@whitehouse.gov
Al Gore	vice-president@whitehouse.gov
Newt Gingrich	georgia6@hr.house.gov
Comments on House of Representatives E-mail service	comments@hr.house.gov
For help on receiving e-mail information from the House of Representatives	househlp@hr.house.gov

Before you e-mail members of Congress, they ask that you mail them a postcard with your own address on it, so that they can verify your congressional district. And as often as not, you'll get your response by the U.S. mail. They say that's to protect privacy, but we figure it's because they can't figure out how to use the e-mail system.

101. I downloaded a game from an online service, but I can't seem to run it. The file is named DESCENT.ZIP. What's wrong with it?

—Locked Out in Lake City

Nothing's wrong with it. You've downloaded a ZIP file. Files with the "ZIP" extension have been "compressed" into a package that takes up half the space to save you time downloading it. The trick is, you have to "unzip" a zipped file before using it.

To do that you need a handy little program called PKZIP.EXE. PKZIP was written by a company called PKWare and is widely available online. Or you can order it from PKWare, 9025 North Deerwood Drive, Brown Deer, WI 53223, or download it from their bulletin board system at (414) 354-8670. PKZip is a shareware program. That means that the authors have made it freely available for evaluation. But they expect you to pay for it if you use it. PKWare also makes a free program called PKUnZip that decompresses but does not compress ZIP files.

Although ZIP files are by far the most common compressed files on-line, there are some other kinds you should be aware of, including ARC, LHA, and ZOO files. Systems that serve up files with these extensions should make available the software to decompress them as well.

In the Macintosh world the most common form of compression is Stuffit. Stuffed files usually have .SIT appended to their names so you'll know they're compressed. Stuffit is also widely available on-line. Or you can order it from

WASHINGTON GOES ONLINE

If you can access the World Wide Web on the Internet, you can find extensive information on pending legislation and more through the THOMAS Legislative Index run by the Library of Congress. Its address is http://thomas.loc.gov.

The House of Representatives has a Web page at http://www.house.gov. You'll find a complete directory of members there. There's currently no Web page for the Senate, but we bet they'll catch up soon.

You can reach the Executive Branch at http://www.whitehouse.gov.

Both the House and Senate offer access to legislation and more through the gopher servers at gopher.house.gov or gopher.senate.gov.

Aladdin Systems at (408) 761-6200, or via e-mail at aladdin@well.com. Aladdin makes a variety of Stuffit models, some commercial, some shareware, and the free Stuffit Expander which, like PKUnZip, expands stuffed files but won't compress them. If all you're doing is downloading software, that's all you'll need.

> *Files with the "ZIP" extension are just files that someone has compressed so it's easier to download and copy. But to run or view it, you've got to "unzip" it first.*

There's another kind of compressed file that can be created by either PKZip or Stuffit, and that's the "self-extracting archive." These files are programs. When you run them they explode into the individual uncompressed component files. Self-extracting PKZip files have the extension .EXE. Self-extracting Stuffit files usually have the extention .SEA. The advantage of self-extracting files is that the end-user doesn't need to have the special decompression software. The disadvantage is that they're slightly larger than the plain ZIP or SIT files.

ZIP and SIT files are so common online that it's usually assumed you'll have the software to expand these files. If you spend a lot of time downloading software from online services, it's a good idea to get the decompression software for yourself.

Lately, online services have been building compression and decompression into their software. If you use CompuServe's Information Manager (CIM) or America Online, they'll automatically compress files before you upload them, and decompress them on download. As long as the online services continue to adhere to the standard forms of compression, ZIP and SIT, we think that's a great idea.

APPENDIX A:
ZiffNet's Black
Book of Tech
Support Numbers

Get Help When You Need It

The Tech Support Little Black Book from ZiffNet helps you get in touch with tech support at nearly 100 of the largest U.S. computer hardware and software companies. The numbers listed in this appendix are also available on ZiffNet as a Windows Help File, which makes searching for information about a company very easy—you just click on the company name to see all the tech support information about that company. You can store the Help file directly on your Windows desktop for easy accessibility. To join ZiffNet and get electronic access to this tech support information, call 800-621-1258 in the continental U.S. or 614-457-8650 elsewhere. If you already have ZiffNet access, you can download the Tech Support Little Black Book from Library 1, General Files of Executives Online Forum (GO EXEC).

All numbers, addresses, and hours of support were correct as of December, 1994. However, this information is subject to change without notice. Fax numbers are main fax numbers unless indicated as tech-support faxes. Faxes sent to these main fax numbers and marked as technical support issues will be routed to the correct department. In some instances, a fax or direct-dial number will only be given out once a support technician has been assigned to your problem.

For the largest companies, all product-specific support numbers have been listed. However, for all other companies, unless otherwise indicated, only a main technical support number, fax number, or BBS number is listed. If the particular company does have more than one support number for either hardware or software, the number we have listed here will be your best source for those secondary listings.

ACER AMERICA CORP.
Subsidiary of The Acer Group
2641 Orchard Pkwy.
San Jose, CA 95134
Main: 408-432-6200; 800-733-2237
Tech support: 800-637-7000
Support hours: 24 hrs/day; 7 days/week
Fax: 408-432-6221
CompuServe: GO PCVENF
BBS: 800-637-7000

ADAPTEC, INC.
691 S. Milpitas Blvd.
Milpitas, CA 95035
Main: 800-959-7274; 408-945-8600
Tech support: 408-945-2550
Support hours: 6am–5pm M–Th; 6am–3pm F
    (PST)
Fax: 408-262-2533
FaxBack Service: 408-957-7150
BBS: 408-945-7727

ADOBE SYSTEMS, INC. & ALDUS CORP.
PO Box 7900, 1585 Charleston Rd.
Mountain View, CA 94039-7900
Main: 800-833-6687; 415-961-4400
Tech support: 408-986-6530
Support hours: 6am–6pm M–F (PST)
Adobe FAX FYI: 206-626-5737
FAX FYI for Type: 206-628-2757
CompuServe: GO ADOBE

ALDUS CORP. (merged with ADOBE CORP.
    September 1, 1994)
Main: 800-333-2538; 206-622-5500
Fax: 206-343-3360
Consumer Division: 619-558-6000
Gallery Effects: 206-628-4507
PageMaker: 206-628-4531
Freehand: 206-628-4532
Persuasion: 206-628-4533
Photostyler: 206-628-4537
Support hours: 7am–5pm M–F (PST)
CompuServe: GO ALDUSFORUM

ADVANCED LOGIC RESEARCH, INC. (ALR)
9401 Jeronimo Rd.
Irvine, CA 92718
Main: 714-581-6770
Tech support: 714-458-0863
Support hours: 6am–6pm M–F;
    7am–1pm S (PST)
Tech fax: 714-458-0532
BBS: 714-458-6834

APPLE COMPUTER, INC.
20525 Mariani Ave.
Cupertino, CA 95014
Main: 408-996-1010
Tech support: 800-776-2333
Support hours: 6am–6pm M–F (PST)
Tech fax: 408-974-9974
CompuServe: GO APPLE

AST RESEARCH INC.
16215 Alton Pkwy., PO Box 57005
Irvine, CA 92619-7005
Main: 800-876-4AST (4278); 714-727-4141
Tech support: 800-727-1278
Support hours: 6am–4:45pm M–F (PST)
Tech fax: 714-727-8579
CompuServe: GO NVENA
BBS: 714-727-4723

ATI TECHNOLOGIES, INC.
33 Commerce Valley Dr., E
Thornhill, ON, CD L3T 7N6
Main: 905-882-2600
Tech support: 905-882-2626
Support hours: 9am–7pm M–F (EST)
Tech fax: 905-882-0546
CompuServe: GO ATITECH (Graphics A Forum)
BBS: 905-764-9404

BANYAN SYSTEMS, INC.
120 Flanders Rd.
Westboro, MA 01581-1033
Main: 508-898-1000
Tech support is provided by resellers.
For basic questions call 508-366-6089.
Support hours: 8am–8pm M-F (EST)
Tech fax: 508-898-9611

Q/A

CompuServe: GO BANYAN
BBS: 508-836-1834; 508-836-1822

BOCA RESEARCH, INC.
6413 Congress Ave.
Boca Raton, FL 33487-2841
Main: 407-997-6227
Tech support: 407-241-8088
Support hours: 8am–7pm M–F (EST)
Tech fax: 407-997-0918
CompuServe: GO BOCA (Modem vendor forum)
BBS: 407-241-1601

BORLAND INTERNATIONAL, INC.
PO Box 660001, 100 Borland Way
Scotts Valley, CA 95067-0001
Main: 408-431-1000
Tech support: 800-523-7070; 408-841-8180
C, C++: 408-461-9133
Pascal: 408-461-9177
Dbase: 408-461-9060
Paradox for DOS: 408-461-9155
Paradox for Windows: 408-461-9166
Quattro Pro for DOS: 408-461-9122
Quattro Pro for Windows: 408-461-9188
Support hours: 6am–5pm M–F (PST)
CompuServe: GO BORLAND
BBS: 408-431-5096
FaxBack: 800-822-4269

BROTHER INTERNATIONAL CORP.
Office Systems Division
200 Cottontail Lane
Somerset, NJ 08875-6714
Main: 908-356-8880
Tech support: 901-373-6256
Fax Machine Tech support: 800-284-4329
Support hours: 9am–4:30pm M–F (CST)
Tech fax: 800-947-1445
BBS: Call main # for listing
Printers:
15 Music
Irvine, CA 92718
Tech Support: 800-276-7746 (outside CA)
 714-859-9700 (in CA)
Support hours: 6am–4pm M–F (PST)
BBS: 714-859-2610

CABLETRON SYSTEMS, INC.
35 Industrial Way, PO Box 5005
Rochester, NH 03867-0505
Main: 603-332-9400
Tech support: 800-332-9401
Support hours: 8am–8pm M–F (EST)
Tech fax: 603-337-3075
BBS: 603-335-4751

CANON COMPUTER SYSTEMS, INC.
Subsidiary of Canon, Inc.
2995 Redhill Ave.
Costa Mesa, CA 92628-5048
Main: 714-438-3000; 800-848-4123
Tech support: 800-423-2366
Support hours: 24 hrs/day, 7 days/wk
Fax: 714-438-3099
CompuServe: GO CANON
BBS: 714-438-3325

CENTRAL POINT SOFTWARE, INC.
Division of Symantec Corp.
(See also WordStar International Corp.)
15220 N.W. Greenbrier Pkwy., Ste. 150
Beaverton, OR 97006
Main: 503-690-8088
Tech support: 800-846-5756; 503-690-8080
PCTools: 503-690-8080
PCTools for Windows: 503-645-6111
Macintosh products: 503-629-9440
Stand Alone Anti-Virus: 503-531-8555
Support hours: 6am–5pm M, T, Th, F;
   6am–4pm W (PST)
Tech fax: 503-690-7133
America Online: CENTRAL
CompuServe: GO CENTRAL
BBS: 503-690-6650 (2,400 bps)
   503-690-4777 (9,600 bps)
FaxBack: 503-690-2660

CITIZEN AMERICA CORP.
Subsidiary of Citizen Watch Co., Ltd.
PO Box 4003, 2450 Broadway, Ste. 600
Santa Monica, CA 90411-4003
Main: 800-477-4683; 310-453-0614
Tech support: 310-453-0614, ext. 464
Support hours: 8am–5pm M–F (PST)

Q/A

Fax: 310-453-2814
BBS: 310-453-7564

CLARIS CORP.
Subsidiary of Apple Computer, Inc.
PO Box 58199, 5201 Patrick Henry Dr.
Santa Clara, CA 95052-8168
Main: 408-987-7000
Tech support: 408-727-9054 (MAC)
 408-727-9004 (WINDOWS)
Support hours: 6am–6pm M–Th;
   6am–2pm F (PST)
Tech fax: 408-987-7447
CompuServe: GO CLARIS
BBS: 408-987-7421

CMS RESEARCH, INC.
627 Bay Shore Dr.
Oshkosh, WI 54901
Main: 414-235-3356
Tech support: 414-235-3356
Support hours: 8am–4:30pm M–F (CST)
Fax: 414-235-3816

COMPAQ COMPUTER CORP.
PO Box 692000
Houston, TX 77269
Main: 713-370-0670; 800-345-1518
Tech support: 800-345-1518
Support hours: 24 hours/day; 7 days/week
Tech fax: 713-378-1442
CompuServe: GO COMPAQ
BBS: 713-378-1418

COMPUSERVE INFORMATION NETWORK
50000 Arlington Centre Blvd.
Columbus, OH 43220
Tech support: 800-848-8990
Support hours: 24 hours/day; 7 days/week
CompuServe: GO SUPPORT

COMPUTER ASSOCIATES INTERNATIONAL, INC.
One Computer Associates Plaza
Islandia, NY 11788-7000
Main: 800-CALL-CAI (225-5224); 516-342-5224
Tech support: check with main number
Support hours: 8am–8pm M–F (EST)

CTX INTERNATIONAL, INC.
20530 Earlgate St.
Walnut, CA 91789
Main: 909-595-6146
Tech support: 800-288-3612; 909-598-8094
Support hours: 9am–5pm M–F (PST)
Tech fax: 201-797-7603

DATA GENERAL CORP.
4400 Computer Dr.
Westboro, MA 01580
Main: 508-366-8911; 800-328-2436
Tech support: 800-344-3577
Support hours: 24 hours/day; 7 days/week

DIGITAL EQUIPMENT CORP. (DEC)
146 Main St.
Maynard, MA 01754-2571
Main: 508-493-5111; 800-332-4636
DEC Direct: 800-344-4825
Tech support: 800-354-9000
Support hours: 24 hours/day; 7 days/week
Fax: 508-841-6100
CompuServe: GO DEC
BBS: 508-496-8800

DELL COMPUTER CORPORATION
9505 Arboretum Blvd.
Austin, TX 78759-7299
Main: 512-338-4400
Tech support: 800-624-9896
Support hours: 24 hours/day; 7 days/week
CompuServe: GO NVENA
BBS: 512-728-8528
FaxBack: 800-950-1329

EPSON AMERICA, INC.
Subsidiary of Seiko Epson Corp.
20770 Madrona Ave., PO Box 2842
Torrance, CA 90509-2842
Main: 310-782-0770; 800-289-3776
Tech support: 800-922-8911 [Printers]
Support hours: 6am–6pm M–F (PST)
CompuServe: GO EPSON
BBS: 310-782-4531

Q/A

EVEREX SYSTEMS, INC.
901 Page Ave.
Fremont, CA 94538
Main: 800-821-0806; 510-498-1111
Tech support: 510-498-4411
Support hours: 6am–5pm M–F (PST)
Tech fax: 510-683-3398
BBS: 510-226-9694

FIFTH GENERATION SYSTEMS, INC.
Subsidiary of Symantec Corp.
10049 N. Reiger Rd.
Baton Rouge, LA 70809-4562
Main: 504-291-7221; 800-677-1848
Tech support:
    Fastback/Direct Access: 503-465-8420
    Disklock/Save: 503-465-8484
    Public Utilities/Doubler Products:
    503-465-8440
Support hours: 7am–7pm M–F (CST)
CompuServe: GO FIFTH
BBS: 504-295-3344 (2,400 bps)
  504-295-3261 (9,600 bps)

FUJITSU COMPUTER PRODUCTS OF
    AMERICA, INC.
Subsidiary of Fujitsu America, Inc.
2904 Orchard Pkwy.
San Jose, CA 95134-2009
Main: 408-432-6333
Tech support: 800-826-6112, 408-894-3950
Support hours: 8am–5pm M–F (PST)
Tech fax: 408-894-3743
CompuServe: GO PACVEN; PCVENJ
BBS: 408-944-9899

GATEWAY 2000, INC.
610 Gateway Dr., PO Box 2000
North Sioux City, SD 57049-2000
Main: 605-232-2000; 800-846-2000
Tech support: 800-846-2301
Support hours: 6am–midnight M–F;
    9am–2pm S (CST)
Tech fax: 605-357-1056
CompuServe: GO GATEWAY
BBS: 605-232-2109 (2,400 bps)
  605-232-2224 (9,600 bps)

HEWLETT-PACKARD CO.
3000 Hanover St.
Palo Alto, CA 94304
Main: 415-857-1501; 800-387-3867
Tech support: 208-323-2551 (printers)
  800-858-8867 (PCs)
Support hours: 7am–6pm M, T, Th, F;
    7am–4pm W (MST)
CompuServe: GO HP

HITACHI AMERICA, LTD.
    (COMPUTER DIVISION)
2000 Sierra Point Pkwy., Hitachi Plaza
Brisbane, CA 94005
Main: 415-589-8300; 800-HITACHI
    (800-448-2244)
Tech support: 800-448-2244
Support hours: 7am–6pm M–F (PST)
BBS: Call for product-specific number

HYUNDAI ELECTRONICS AMERICA
Subsidiary of Hyundai Electronics Industries
    Co. Ltd.
166 Baypointe Pkwy.
San Jose, CA 95134
Main: 800-727-6972; 408-473-9200
Tech support: 800-289-4986
Support hours: 7am–5pm M–F (PST)
Fax: 800-964-4762
BBS: 408-473-9899

IBM (INTERNATIONAL BUSINESS MACHINES)
Old Orchard Rd.
Armonk, NY 10504
Main: 914-765-1900
Tech support: 800-722-2227
Support hours: 6am–6pm M–F (MST); 24
    hours/day; 7 days/week for BBS
CompuServe: GO IBMNET
BBS: 919-517-0001
Fax Info System: 800-426-3395

INTEL CORP.
PO Box 58119, 2200 Mission College Blvd.
Santa Clara, CA 95052-8119
Main: 408-765-8080
Tech support: 800-628-8686 [Components and
    microprocessors]
  503-629-7000 [PC & LAN Enhancements
    Division]
Support hours: 7am–5pm M–F (PST)
CompuServe: GO INTEL
BBS: [Components] 800-897-2536 view only
  916-356-3600 download
[Branded products] 503-645-6275

INTUIT
PO Box 3014
Menlo Park, CA 94026
Main: 415-322-0573; 415-852-9696
Tech support: 800-624-8742
Support hours: 7am–5pm M–F (PST)
CompuServe: GO INTUIT

KODAK LABORATORY RESEARCH PRODUCTS
Division of Eastman Kodak Co.
25 Science Park, PO Box 9558
New Haven, CT 06511
Main: 800-243-2555; 203-786-5600
Tech support: 800-243-2555
Support hours: 8:30am–5pm M–F (EST)
Fax: 203-624-3143
CompuServe: GO KODAK

LEADING EDGE PRODUCTS, INC.
Subsidiary of Daewoo Telecom, Ltd. Co.
117 Flanders Rd., PO Box 5020
Westborough, MA 01581-5020
Main: 800-874-3340; 508-836-4800
Tech support: 900-370-4800
Support hours: 9am–5:30pm M–F (PST)
Fax: 508-836-4504
BBS: 508-836-3967

LOGITECH, INC.
6505 Kaiser Drive
Fremont, CA 94555
Main: 800-231-7717; 510-795-8500
Tech Support: 510-795-8100

Support hours: 8am–5pm M–Th;
    9am–4pm F, S, S (PST)
Tech fax: 510-505-0978
CompuServe: GO LOGITECH
BBS: 510-795-0408

LOTUS DEVELOPMENT CORP.
55 Cambridge Pkwy.
Cambridge, MA 02142-1295
Main: 617-577-8500; 800-343-5414
1st minute free/$2 each additional minute:
    900-454-9009
Automated support center: 800-346-3508
No Prompt ID #; call to renew contract:
    800-553-4270
The following support services require a Prompt
    ID number:
Windows (with Prompt ID #): 800-386-8600
DOS (with Prompt ID #): 800-223-1662
Ami Pro 2.0 and 3.0: 800-386-8600
Ami Pro 3.1: 404-399-5505
cc:Mail: 415-966-4900
Notes: 800-437-6391
Support hours: 24 hours/day; 7 days/week
Fax: 617-693-3512
CompuServe: GO LOTUS

MAG INNOVISION
2801 South Yale St.
Santa Ana, CA 92704
Main: 800-827-3998
Tech support: 714-751-2008
Support hours: 8am–5pm M–F (PST)

MICROSOFT CORP.
One Microsoft Way
Redmond, WA 98052-6399
Main: 206-882-8080
FastTips: 800-936-3500
Fax: Call main number for product-specific fax
    tech support

STANDARD SUPPORT
Desktop Programs for Windows
Access: 206-635-7050
Excel for Windows and OS/2: 206-635-7070
FoxPro Products for Windows: 206-635-7191

Q/A

Money: 206-635-7131
Multimedia Products: 206-635-7172
Office for Windows: 206-635-7056
PowerPoint: 206-635-7145
Profit (supported by Great Plains Software):
    800-723-3333
Project: 206-635-7155
Publisher: 206-635-7140
Schedule+: 206-635-7049
Video for Windows: 206-635-7172
Windows Entertainment Products: 206-637-9308
Word for Windows: 206-462-9673
Works for Windows: 206-635-7130

Desktop Programs for MS-DOS
FoxPro Products for MS-DOS: 206-635-7191
Word for MS-DOS: 206-635-7210
Works for MS-DOS: 206-635-7150

Desktop Programs for the Macintosh
Excel for the Macintosh: 206-635-7080
FoxPro Products for the Macintosh: 206-635-7192
Office for the Macintosh: 206-635-7055
Word for the Macintosh: 206-635-7200
Works for the Macintosh: 206-635-7160
Personal Operating Systems and Hardware:
Windows: 206-635-7040: 206-637-7098
Windows for Workgroups: 206-637-7098
MS-DOS 6 and 6.2 Upgrade: 206-646-5104

Advanced Systems
Windows NT: 206-635-7018

PRIORITY 900-NUMBER SUPPORT:
Desktop ($2/minute, $25/incident cap):
    900-555-2000
Personal Operating Systems ($2/minute,
    $25/incident cap): 900-555-2000
Development with Desktop ($2/minute,
    $25/incident cap): 900-555-2300
Comprehensive ($150/incident): 900-555-2100

PRIORITY CREDIT-CARD SUPPORT
Desktop ($25/incident): 800-936-5700
Personal Operating Systems ($25/incident):
    800-936-5700
Development with Desktop ($95/incident):
    800-936-5800
Comprehensive ($150/incident): 800-936-5900

FAST TIPS AND ELECTRONIC SERVICES
Desktop Applications FastTips: 800-936-4100
Personal Operating Systems FastTips:
    800-936-4200
Development FastTips: 800-936-4300
Advanced Systems FastTips: 800-936-4400
Microsoft Download Service: 206-936-6735
CompuServe Information Service Sales:
    800-848-8199
Support hours: 6am–6pm M–F (PST)
CompuServe: GO MICROSOFT

MITSUBISHI ELECTRONICS AMERICA, INC.
Display Products Division
5665/5757 Plaza Dr., PO Box 6007
Cypress, CA 90630-0007
Main: 800-843-2515; 714-220-2500
Tech support: 800-344-6352
Support hours: 8am–11:50am;
    12:30pm–4:30pm M–F (PST)
Tech fax: 714-236-6425
FaxBack: 714-236-6453
BBS: 714-236-6286

MOTOROLA, INC.
1303 E. Algonquin Rd.
Schaumburg, IL 60196
Main: 708-576-5000
Tech support: 800-521-6274 (chips)
Support hours: 7:30am–4pm (MST)

NANAO USA CORP.
23535 Telo Ave.
Torrance, CA 90505
Main: 310-325-5202
Tech Support: 310-325-5202, ext. 114
Support hours: 8:30am–5pm M–F (PST)
Fax: 310-530-1679
BBS: 310-325-4744

NATIONAL SEMICONDUCTOR CORP.
PO Box 58090, 2900 Semiconductor Dr.
Santa Clara, CA 95052-8090
Main: 408-721-5000
Tech support: 800-272-9959
Support hours: 7am–5pm M–F (PST)
Tech fax: 800-428-0065

NCR CORP.
1700 S. Patterson Blvd.
Dayton, OH 45479
Main: 513-445-5000
Tech support: 800-543-9935
Support hours: 24 hrs/day; 7 days/week
CompuServe: GO NCR
BBS: 800-624-5672 (EasyLink)
   800-325-4112 (Direct dial)

NEC TECHNOLOGIES INC.
1414 Mass. Ave.
Boxborough, MA 01719
Main: 508-264-8000
Tech support: 800-388-8888
Support hours: 8:30am–8pm M–F (CST)
Fax: 508-635-4666
FaxBack: 800-366-0476
BBS: 508-635-4706

NORTHGATE COMPUTER SYSTEMS, INC.
PO Box 208
Chaska, MN 55318
Main: 800-548-1996; 612-361-5000
Tech support: 800-446-5037
Support hours: 24 hrs./day; 7 days/week
Tech fax: 612-361-5219
CompuServe: GO PCVENA
BBS: 612-361-5201 (2400 bps)
   612-361-5217 (9600 bps)

NOVELL, INC.
122 East 1700 South
Provo, UT 84606-6194
Main: 800-453-1267; 801-429-7000
Tech support: 800-638-9273 (800-Netware)
Support hours: 24 hrs/day; 7 days/week
Tech fax: 801-429-5200
CompuServe: GO NOVELL
BBS: 800-848-8199

OKIDATA CORP.
Division of OKI America, Inc.
532 Fellowship Rd.
Mt. Laurel, NJ 08054
Main: 800-654-3282; 609-235-2600
Tech support: 609-273-0300

Support hours: 8am–6pm M–F (EST)
Tech fax: 609-273-2779
BBS: 800-283-5474

OLIVETTI NORTH AMERICA
Subsidiary of Olivetti Co.
Systems software/applications/computer systems
22425 E. Appleway Ave.
Liberty Lake, WA 99019-9534
Main: 800-633-9909; 509-927-5600
Tech support: 800-525-3991
Support hours: 8:30am–5pm M–F (EST)
Tech fax: 509-927-5759

PACKARD BELL, INC.
9425 Canoga Ave.
Chatsworth, CA 91311
Main: 818-886-9998
Tech support: 800-733-4411; 801-579-0161
Support hours: 8am–5pm M–F (PST)
Fax: 818-773-9516
CompuServe: GO PACKARDBELL

PANASONIC COMMUNICATIONS & SYSTEMS CO.
Office Automation Group
2 Panasonic Way
Secaucus, NJ 07094
Main: 800-742-8086; 201-392-4500
Tech support: 800-222-0584
Support hours: 9am–5pm M–F (EST)

PRODIGY INTERACTIVE PERSONAL SERVICE
445 Hamilton Avenue
White Plains, NY 10601
Main: 914-448-8000
Tech support: 800-PRODIGY (776-3449)
Support hours: 24 hours/day; 7 days/week

PROTEON, INC.
9 Technology Dr.
Westborough, MA 01581-1799
Main: 508-898-2800
Tech support: 508-898-2800
Support hours: 8am–8pm M–F (EST)
Tech fax: 508-898-2118
BBS: 508-366-7827

PURE DATA, INC.
1333 Corporate Drive, Ste. 200
Irving, TX 75030
Main: 800-661-8210; 214-242-2040
Tech support: 800-661-8210
Support hours: 8am–8pm M–F (CST)
Tech fax: 905-731-4137
CompuServe: GO PUREDATA
BBS: 416-492-5980

QMS, INC.
One Magnum Pass, PO Box 81250
Mobile, AL 36689-1250
Main: 205-633-4300
Tech support: 205-633-4500
Support hours: 7am–6pm M–F (CST)
Tech fax: 205-633-3716
BBS: 205-633-3632

QUALITAS, INC.
7101 Wisconsin Ave., Ste. 1386
Bethesda, MD 20814
Main: 301-907-6700
Tech support: 301-907-7400
Support hours: 10am–5pm M–F (EST)
Tech fax: 301-718-6061
FaxBack: 301-718-6061
CompuServe: GO PCVENA

QUARTERDECK OFFICE SYSTEMS
150 Pico Blvd.
Santa Monica, CA 90405-1018
Main: 800-354-3222; 310-392-9851
Tech support: 310-392-9701
Support hours: 7:30am–4:30pm M–Th;
    10am–4:30pm F (PST)
Tech fax: 310-314-3217
CompuServe: GO QUARTERDECK
BBS: 310-314-3227

QUE SOFTWARE
Division of Macmillan Computer Publishing
11711 N. College Ave., Ste. 140
Carmel, IN 46032-5634
Main: 800-992-0244; 317-581-3500
Tech support: 317-581-3833
Support hours: 9am–5pm M–F (CST)

Fax: 317-581-4773
CompuServe: GO MACMILLAN
BBS: 317-581-4771

RADIUS
215 Moffat Ave.
Sunnyvale, CA 94089
Main: 408-541-6100
Tech support: 408-541-6100
Support hours: 9am–5pm M–F (PST)
Tech fax: 408-541-5834
CompuServe: GO RADIUS
BBS: 408-531-6190

SAMTRON DISPLAYS, INC.
Division of Samsung Display Devices Co., Ltd.
18600 Broadwich St.
Rancho Domingo, CA 90220
Main: 310-537-7000, ext. 2010
Tech support: 310-537-7000
Support hours: 8am–5pm M–F (PST)
Tech fax: 310-537-1033

SEIKO INSTRUMENTS U.S.A., INC.
Printers, monitors:
1130 Ringwood Ct.
San Jose, CA 95131
Main: 408-922-5900
Tech support: 800-553-5312
Support hours: 7am–5pm M–F (PST)
Fax: 408-922-5840
BBS: 408-428-9810

SEIKOSHA AMERICA, INC.
10 Industrial Ave.
Mahwah, NJ 07430
Main: 800-338-2609; 201-327-7227
Tech support: 800-825-5349
Support hours: 6am–midnight M–F (PST)

SHIVA CORP.
63 Third Ave., Northwest Park
Burlington, MA 01803
Main: 617-270-8300
Tech support: 617-270-8400
Support hours: 9am–6pm M–F (EST)
Tech fax: 617-270-8599
BBS: 617-273-0023

**SIEMENS NIXDORF INFORMATION
    SYSTEMS, INC.**
Applications:
200 Wheeler Rd.
Burlington, MA 01803
Main: 800-225-1484; 617-273-0480
Tech support: 617-273-0480
Support hours: 8am–5pm M–F (EST)
Tech fax: 617-221-0215
Corporate headquarters: Q 212-258-4000

SIEMENS NIXDORF PRINTING SYSTEMS, LP
Printers:
5500 Broken Sound Blvd.
Boca Raton, FL 33487-3599
Main: 800-523-5444; 407-997-3100
Tech support: 407-997-3100
Support hours: 8am–4:45pm M–F (EST)
Tech fax: 407-997-2924

SOFTKEY INTERNATIONAL
(Formerly Spinnaker Software Corp.)
(See also WordStar International Corp.)
201 Broadway, 6th Fl.
Cambridge, MA 02139-1901
Main: 800-323-8088; 617-494-1200
Tech support: 404-428-0008
Support hours: 10am–5pm M–F (EST)
Tech fax: 617-494-0119
CompuServe: GO SPINNAKER

SOFTWARE PUBLISHING CORP. (SPC)
3165 Kifer Rd., PO Box 54983
Santa Clara, CA 95056-0983
Main: 408-986-8000
Tech support: 408-988-4005; 800-234-2500
Support hours: 7am–4pm M–F (PST)
Tech fax: 408-980-1518
CompuServe: GO SPC
BBS: 408-986-0342 (2,400 bps)
    408-986-1272 (9,600 bps)

SONY CORP. OF AMERICA
Computer Peripheral Products Co.
3300 Zanker Rd.
San Jose, CA 95134
Main: 800-352-7669; 408-432-0190

Tech support: 408-894-0555 (end users)
Support hours: 8am–5pm M–F (PST)
Tech fax: 408-955-5169
BBS: 408-955-5107

STAC ELECTRONICS
12636 Five Bluff Dr.
San Diego, CA 92130-3400
Main: 619-431-7474
Tech support: 619-929-3900
Support hours: 8am–5pm M–F (PST)
CompuServe: GO STACKER
BBS: 619-431-5956
FaxBack: 619-431-8585

STANDARD MICROSYSTEMS CORP.
System Products Division
80 Arkay Dr.
Hauppauge, NY 11788
Main: 516-435-6000; 800-SMC-4-YOU
    (762-4968)
TECH SUPPORT: 800-992-4762
Support hours: 8:30am–8pm M–F (EST)
Tech fax: 516-434-9314
CompuServe: GO SMC
BBS: 516-434-3162 (East Coast)
    714-707-2481 (West Coast)

STAR MICRONICS AMERICA, INC.
Subsidiary of Star Micronics Co. Ltd.
70 Ethel Road West
Paskataway, NJ 08854
Main: 908-572-5550
Tech support: 908-572-3300
Support hours: 10am–6pm M; 9am–6pm T–Th
    (EST)
Tech fax: 908-572-5995
FaxBack: 908-572-4004
BBS: 908-572-5010

SYMANTEC CORP.
10201 Torre Ave.
Cupertino, CA 95014-2132
Main: 800-441-7234; 408-253-9600
Tech support: 503-465-8600
Support hours: 7am–5pm M–F (PST)
Fax: 503-334-7473

FaxBack: 800-554-4403
CompuServe: GO SYMANTEC
BBS: 503-484-6699 (2,400 bps)
   503-484-6669 (9,600 bps)

SYNOPTICS COMMUNICATIONS, INC.
PO Box 58185
4401 Great America Pkwy.
Santa Clara, CA 95052-8185
Main: 408-988-2400
Tech support: 800-473-4911
Support hours: 7am–5:30pm M–F (PST)
Tech fax: 408-764-1188
CompuServe: GO NVENA

TANDY CORP./RADIO SHACK
700 One Tandy Center
Ft. Worth, TX 76102
Main: 817-390-3011
Tech support: 817-390-3861
Support hours: 9am–7pm M–F (CST)
Tech fax: 817-870-0412
CompuServe: GO TANDY

TEXAS INSTRUMENTS, INC.
Hardware:
PO Box 655474
Dallas, TX 75265
Main: 800-527-3500; 214-995-2011
Tech support: 800-336-5236
Support hours: 7:30am–5:30pm M–F (CST)
CompuServe: GO TIFORUM

TEXAS INSTRUMENTS, INC. (INFORMATION TECH. GROUP)
Software applications:
6550 Chase Oaks Blvd., M/S 8411
Plano, TX 75086
Main: 800-336-5236; 214-995-2011
Tech Support: 800-336-5236
Support hours: 7:30am–5:30pm M–F (CST)
CompuServe: GO TIFORUM

3COM CORP.
PO Box 58145
5400 Bayfront Plaza
Santa Clara, CA 95052-8145

Main: 408-764-5000
Tech support: 800-876-3266
Support hours: 8am–6pm M–F (PST)
CompuServe: Go ASKFORUM
BBS: 408-980-8204

TOSHIBA AMERICA CONSUMER PRODUCTS, INC.
17" and 21" monitors only: Softkey International, formerly Spinnaker Software Corp.— see also WordStar International Corp.
201 Broadway, 6th Fl.
Cambridge, MA 02139-1901
Main: 800-323-8088; 617-494-1200
Tech support: 404-428-0008
Support hours: 10am–5pm M–F (EST)
Tech fax: 617-494-0119
CompuServe: GO SPINNAKER
All other products:
1010 Johnson Dr.
Buffalo Grove, IL 60089-6900
Main: 800-253-5429; 708-541-9400
Tech support: 708-541-9400, ext. 232
Support hours: 9am–12pm; 1pm–5pm M-F (CST)
CompuServe: GO TOSHIBA

TOSHIBA AMERICA INFORMATION SYSTEMS, INC. (TAIS)
Subsidiary of Toshiba Corp.
Notebooks:
9740 Irvine Blvd., PO Box 19724
Irvine, CA 92718
Main: 800-334-3445; 714-583-3000
Tech support: 714-587-9476
Support hours: 8am–4pm M–F (PST)
Tech fax: 714-583-3827

VIEWSONIC
20480 Business Pkwy.
Walnut, CA 91789
Main: 909-869-7976
Tech support: 909-869-7976
Support hours: 8am–5pm M–F (PST)
Fax: 909-869-7958
BBS: 909-468-1241

Q/A

WORDPERFECT CORP.
1555 N. Technology Way
Orem, UT 84057-2399
Main: 800-451-5151; 801-225-5000
Tech fax: 801-222-4377
Tech support: 800-451-5151 (for product-
    specific numbers)
WordPerfect for Windows 6.0
Features: 800-228-9907
Graphics and Tables: 800-228-8720
Macro/merge/labels: 800-228-2021
Laser printers/Postscript/Bitstream: 800-228-2803
Dot matrix printers: 800-228-6646
Installation: 800-228-7610
Networks: 800-228-8807
WordPerfect for DOS 6.0
Features: 800-228-9038
Graphics and tables: 800-228-9006
Macro/merge/labels: 800-228-9013
Laser printers/Postscript/Bitstream: 800-228-9027
Dot matrix printers: 800-228-9032
Installation: 800-228-9012
Networks: 800-228-9019
WordPerfect for Windows 5.2
Features: 800-228-1029
Graphics and tables: 800-228-6013
Macro/merge/labels: 800-228-1032
Laser printers/Postscript/Bitstream: 800-228-1023
Dot matrix printers: 800-228-1017
Installation: 800-228-6076
Networks: 800-228-6066
WordPerfect for DOS 5.2/5.0/4.2
Features: 800-228-5096
Graphics and tables: 800-228-3383
Macro/merge/labels: 800-228-5129
Laser printers/Postscript/Bitstream: 800-228-5170
Dot matrix printers: 800-228-5160
Installation: 800-228-9605
Networks: 800-228-3389
DataPerfect: 800-321-3249
Presentations for DOS/Windows: 800-541-5098
Office for DOS/Windows: 800-321-3253
Informs for DOS/Windows: 801-228-9916
Works: 800-321-3512
WordPerfect for Macintosh: 800-228-2875
DOS/Windows: 801-228-9918
Macintosh: 801-228-9917

Unix: 801-226-5333
Support hours: 7am–6pm M–F (MST)
After-hours support: 801-228-9908
    [6pm–7am M–Th; 6pm–12pm F;
    8am–4pm F (MST)]
CompuServe: GO WORDPERFECT
BBS: 801-225-4414 (2,400 bps)
    801-225-4414 (9,600 bps)

WORDSTAR INTERNATIONAL, INC.
(Also Softkey, Spinnaker, ZSoft, & PowerUp
    Products)
201 Broadway, 6th Fl.
Cambridge, MA 02139-1901
Main: 800-323-8088; 617-494-1200
Tech support: 404-428-0008
Support hours: 9am–6pm M–F (EST)
Tech fax: 404-427-1150
FaxBack: 404-514-6333
CompuServe: GO WORDSTAR
BBS: 404-514-6332

XEROX COMPUTER SERVICES/MDIS
Software applications:
5310 Beethoven St.
Los Angeles, CA 90066
Main: 310-306-4000
Tech support: 310-306-4000
Support hours: 8am–5pm M–F (PST)
BBS: 310-306-1513

XEROX CORP.
U.S. Customer Operations Division
Modems, printers:
PO Box 24
Rochester, NY 14601
Main: 716-423-5078
Tech support: 800-832-6979
Support hours: 8am–7:30pm M–Th;
    8am–6pm F (EST)

XIRCOM, INC.
26025 Mureau Rd.
Calabasas, CA 91302
Main: 818-878-7600
Tech support: 800-874-4428
Support hours: 6am–4:30pm M–F (PST)

Tech fax: 818-878-7175
CompuServe: GO PCVENH
BBS: 818-878-7618

XTREE

Division of Symantec Corp. (see also Wordstar
    International Corp.)
15220 N.W. Greenbrier Pkwy., Ste. 150
Beaverton, OR 97006
Main: 800-964-6896; 503-690-8088
Tech support: 503-690-8080
Support hours: 6am–5pm M–F (PST)
Fax: 503-690-7133
CompuServe: GO CENTRAL
BBS: 503-690-6650 (2,400 bps)
    503-690-4777 (9,600 bps)

ZENITH DATA SYSTEMS

2150 E. Lake Cook Rd.
Buffalo Grove, IL 60089
Main: 708-808-5000
Tech support: 800-227-3360
Support hours: 7am–11pm M–F (CST)
CompuServe: GO ZENITH
BBS: 708-808-4942

ZEOS INTERNATIONAL LTD.

1301 Industrial Blvd.
Minneapolis, MN 55413-9852
Main: 800-423-5891; 612-623-9614
Tech support: 800-228-5390
Support hours: 24 hrs/day; 7 days/wk
Tech fax: 612-633-4607
CompuServe: GO PCVENE

GLOSSARY

16-bit sound

Sound that has been digitized using 16 bits of information per sample. 16-bit sound is CD-quality audio.

8-bit sound

Sound that has been digitized using 8 bits of information per sample. This produces poorer quality digital sound, roughly equivalent to that of an AM radio.

active matrix display

A type of liquid crystal display (LCD) found in better laptops. It offers a crisper picture with much better color saturation than the less expensive passive matrix LCDs.

adapter card

Also known as an add-on card, controller, or I/O card. Adapters are installed in expansion slots to enhance the processing power of the computer or to communicate with other devices. Examples of adapters include asynchronous communication, floppy disk-controllers, and expanded memory.

ADB (Apple desktop bus)

The Macintosh connector used to attach keyboard, mouse, and joysticks.

ALT key

The alternate key on the keyboard is like the Shift key: When used simultaneously with another key it generates a command. In Windows the Alt key is used alone to activate an application's menu.

Alt, Alternate key

See ALT key.

analog

A real world representation of an object, as opposed to the digital representation required by a computer. A record is an analog recording of sound—the grooves in the record represent the sound waves. A CD is a digital recording of the same sound.

ANSI (American National Standards Institute)

An organization that develops and publishes standards for codes, alphabets, and signaling schemes.

antivirus program

A software program that detects and eradicates computer viruses.

Apple Desktop Bus

See ADB.

application software

A computer program designed to help people perform a certain type of work. An application can manipulate text, numbers, graphics, or a combination of elements. Some application packages focus on a single task and offer greater computer power while others, called integrated software, offer less power but include several applications, such as word processing, spreadsheet, and database programs. An application may also be referred to as software, program, instructions, or task.

arrow keys

The keys on a computer keyboard marked with arrow symbols. In a word processing program, the arrow keys are used to move the text insertion point by one character to the left or right, or by one line up or down.

ASCII (American Standard Code for Information Interchange)

The code used internally by computers to represent text. The ASCII character set includes 255 different symbols for the letters of the alphabet, diacritical marks, the numbers 0 through 9, standard punctuation, and graphics symbols.

AT Command Set

See Hayes compatible modem.

AUTOEXEC.BAT

One of the text configuration files loaded by DOS machines during the startup process (like CONFIG.SYS). The startup configuration of your system can be changed by editing this file.

backlit display

A laptop display screen that is lit from behind.

backup

To make a copy of the files on a hard disk in order to preserve them in case of damage to the disk.

baud

An old-fashioned measure of modem transmission speeds. Baud is sometimes erroneously used in place of bits per second.

BBS (bulletin Board System)

A computer (generally a microcomputer) set up to receive calls and act as a host system. BBSs allow users to communicate through message bases and to exchange files.

beta

A version of a program that is distributed to testers before the official release. Beta versions of programs are usually very unreliable and not intended for public consumption.

BIOS (basic input/output system)

A collection of primitive computer routines (stored in ROM in a PC) that control peripherals such as the video display, disk drives, and keyboard.

bit

A binary digit: the smallest piece of information that can be recognized and processed by a computer. A bit is either 0 or 1. Bits can form larger units of information called nibbles (4 bits), bytes (8 bits), and words (usually 16 bits).

bitmapped

A display that is represented in the computer's memory as dots or bits.

boot disk

A disk that can be used to start up the computer.

boot up

To start up the computer.

bps (bits per second)

The number of data bits sent per second between two modems. Used as a measure of the rate at which digital information is handled, manipulated, or transmitted.

break

A signal to the computer to temporarily halt the current process.

browsers

Programs, like Mosaic and Netscape, that provide a graphical interface to the Internet.

bugs

Program errors.

bulletin board systems

See BBS.

burn in

To test a computer by running it for a long period of time in warm conditions. When a computer is hot, its components are more likely to fail.

bus

A group of wires used to carry a set of related signals or information within a computer from one device to another.

byte

A sequence of adjacent binary digits that the computer considers a unit. A byte consists of 8 bits.

cache

An amount of RAM set aside to hold data that is expected to be accessed again.

carpal tunnel syndrome

A repetitive stress injury (RSI) caused by too much typing.

carrier

The continuous signal which carries information between modems.

cathode ray tube

See CRT.

CBT (Computer Based Training)

An interactive computer program that teaches you how to use a different program.

CCITT (Consultative Committee for International Telephone and Telegraph)

Now known as the ITU-TSS (International Telecommunications Union-Telecommunications Standards Section) The international body that sets standards for modems and other communications devices.

CD-ROM (compact-disc read only memory)

A compact disc used to hold up to 650MB of computer data, including programs, graphics, sound, and video.

central processing unit

See CPU.

chat rooms

Online discussion areas where people type to each other in real time.

chip

An integral part of the PC. These are very tiny, square or rectangular slivers of material (usually silicon) with electrical components built in. Some of the chips in a computer act as memory, but the most important chip is the CPU. This is the "8088," "286," "386," or "486" that every salesperson will speak of when talking about a specific machine's features.

clock speed

The speed with which the CPU operates, expressed in mHz.

clock-doubled

A chip that's internal clock speed has been doubled, while the external speed remains the same. A clock-doubled chip can be used as an upgrade because it looks the same to the rest of the computer, but works twice as fast inside.

clone

An IBM PC/XT- or AT-compatible computer made by a manufacturer other than IBM.

cold boot

To restart the computer from the beginning. The same as turning the computer off and on again.

COM ports

PC communications port or serial port used by modems, mice, and some printers. Most PCs come with at least two COM ports.

compression

A technique for reducing the size of computer files by eliminating redundant information.

Q/A

computer based training

See CBT.

connector

A socket or plug that is used to link two computer devices together.

CONTROL Key (CTRL or CTL)

The control key is like the Shift key: When used simultaneously with another key it generates a command. Sometimes abbreviated with a caret (^), as in ^C for Control-C.

controller card

See adapter card.

conventional memory

The first 640K of memory in an IBM-PC compatible computer. This is the most memory DOS programs can access directly.

CPU (central processing unit)

The "brain" of the computer; the element that does the actual adding and subtracting of 0s and 1s and the manipulation and moving of data that is essential to computing.

crash

A hardware or software failure that causes the computer to stop working.

CRT (cathode ray tube)

The tube-based display screen on a desktop computer.

CTRL key

See CONTROL key.

cursor

A symbol on the screen that indicates where the user's next action will take place. On text-based displays, the cursor is often represented by a blinking rectangle or underline mark. On graphical displays, it's often an arrow, hand, or I-beam.

daisy chain

To connect multiple devices together in a series, one after another.

database

A collection of related information that is arranged for easy access. A database program is used to create, manage, and search a computer database.

DB-9

A 9-pin connector, usually for serial ports. The connector attached to your laptop is typically a male DB-9. The device at the other end (an external modem, most likely) almost always has a 25-pin (DB-25) connector and is always female. This means the cable you want to buy is 9-pin female (computer end) to 25-pin male (modem end). Some older laptops with EGA video connectors will have a 9-pin female connector on the laptop.

DB-25

A 25-pin connector for parallel ports and some serial ports (mostly on desktop PCs). At the computer end, the parallel port is female and the serial port is male. At the other end, the connector is a 36-pin Centronics male (parallel) or 25-pin female (serial). For printers, specify a DB-25 male to a Centronics cable. For serial devices, specify a DB-25 female to a DB-25 male cable.

default

The standard configuration. The way a program or piece of hardware was configured at the factory.

defragment

To reorganize a disk so that all the files are stored contiguously. This improves performance.

DELETE

Del (Delete key). In most word processing programs, this key will delete the characters to the right of the cursor.

desktop

In Graphical Operating Systems, the flat space behind all the windows. The area of the screen that is not in a window.

digital

The numeric representation of information.

DIN connector

Plug and socket conforming to the DIN (Deutsche Industrie Norm) standard.

DIP (dual inline package)

The most common form of computer chip. A rectangular chip with leg-like connectors on the long sides which are inserted into sockets on circuit boards.

directory

A list of file names and locations of files on a disk.

disk

A circular metal platter or mylar disk with magnetic material on both sides that stores programs and data. Disks are rotated continuously so that read/write heads mounted on movable or fixed arms can read or write programs or data to and from the disk.

disk cache

A portion of a computer's RAM set aside for temporarily holding information read from a disk. Disk caches improve the performance of your disk drives.

disk compression

To increase the available space on a disk by shrinking the size of the files on it.

disk drive

A device that reads and writes data on a disk to store it.

display

The TV-like screen attached to your computer.

DMA (direct memory access)

A special channel for data transfer between devices that bypasses the CPU.

DOS (disk operating system)

A set of programs that control the communications between components of the computer. Examples of DOS functions are: displaying characters on the screen, reading and writing to a disk, printing, and accepting commands from the keyboard. DOS is a widely used operating system on IBM-compatible personal computers (PCs).

dot matrix printer

A type of printer technology using a print head with pins to poke out arrays of dots that form text and graphics.

dot pitch

> The distance in millimeters between dots on a color computer monitor. The lower the number, the finer the resolution of the monitor and the crisper the display.

double speed

> A CD-ROM drive that turns twice as fast as an audio CD drive. That means that it can transfer twice the data in the same amount of time.

download

> To receive information from another modem and computer over the telephone lines. It is the opposite of upload.

DRAM (dynamic random-access memory)

> The most commonly used type of memory chip. DRAM is usually slower than VRAM (video random-access memory), since it has only a single access pathway.

drawing tablet

> A special input device that lets you use a pen instead of a mouse to draw on the screen.

DSDD (double-sided, double-density)

> DSDD means 720K 3½-inch disks or 360K 5¼-inch disks.

DSHD (double-sided, high-density)

> DSHD (often abbreviated "HD") means 1.44MB 3½-inch disks or 1.2MB 5¼-inch disks.

dual inline packages

> *See* DIP.

DX

> A designation Intel adds to the names of its 386 and 486 chips. On a 386 the DX means it has a full 32-bit data path. On a 486 it means that the chip has a built-in math co-processor.

EGA

> IBM's second graphics standard (1984), capable of 640 by 300 resolution at 16 colors.

electronic mail

See e-mail.

e-mail (electronic mail)

The electronic exchange of messages over a network or online.

END key

When pressed, this key moves the cursor to the bottom of the screen, end of the line, or end of a file.

ENTER key

When pressed, this key lets the computer know a command has been issued; in a word processing document, this key is used like a typewriter's Return key to add a carriage return. Also called the Return key.

ESC key (Escape key)

A key that will usually back you out of a program, a menu, a dialog box, or a command.

escape

See ESC.

expanded memory

Memory above the conventional 640K. Used by some DOS programs.

expansion card

See adapter card.

extended memory

Memory above 1Mb in 80286 and better computers. Can be used for RAM disks, disk caches, or Microsoft Windows.

F1

See function keys.

FAQ (frequently asked questions)

FAQ files contain the answers to often asked questions (just like this book). They are commonly made available online to help beginners get oriented and to save experts from having to answer the same questions over and over.

file

A collection of related records treated as a unit. In a computer system, a file can exist on magnetic tape, disk, or as an accumulation of information in system memory. A file can contain data, programs, or both.

File Manager

A Windows program for managing stored files.

File Transfer Protocol

See FTP.

floppy disk

A removable, rotating, flexible magnetic storage disk. Floppy disks come in a variety of sizes, but 3½-inch and 5¼-inch are the most popular. Storage capacity is usually between 360K and 1.44MB. Also called flexible disk or diskette.

floppy drive

A disk drive designed to read and write data to a floppy disk for transfer to and from a computer.

folders

A metaphor for organizing files on a disk. Files can be categorized into folders, and folders can be stored in other folders hierarchically.

font

A single style in a typeface family. This book is set in the Utopia and Univers typeface families. The text you are reading now is Utopia Regular. The heading is Univers Bold.

format

To prepare a disk for use by recording organizational information on it. It's like drawing lines on a piece of paper before writing on it.

freeware

Software that is given away. Usually the author retains the copyright.

frequently asked questions

See FAQ.

FTP (file transfer protocol)

An Internet protocol for the transfer of files between machines.

function keys (F-keys)

Keys numbered from F1 to F12 that are used to perform special functions. For example, F1 in most software will activate the help screen.

game port

A connector on the back of PCs for attaching joysticks and other game controllers.

general protection fault

See GPF.

gigabyte

One billion bytes.

gopher

A program that provides a menu interface to the Internet.

GPF (General Protection Fault)

A message that indicates that a serious error has occured in a program running under Windows. When you get a GPF error message, it's best to save your work immediately and restart Windows.

graphical user interface

See GUI.

graphics adapters

Add-in circuit boards that drive computer monitors.

GUI (graphical user interface)

A computer user interface that uses menus, windows, icons, and a mouse to make the computer more attractive and easier to use.

hacker

An advanced computer programmer. Often mistakenly used to describe people who break into computer systems.

handshaking

A modem term that describes the initial exchange between modems. It's like "are you there?" with the response "I am here."

hard disk

Also called an internal disk, hard drive, hard-disk drive, or fixed disk. A bulk data storage system with sealed, rotating, magnetic storage disks.

hardware

The physical components of a computer.

Hayes-compatible modem

A modem that uses the industry-standard AT command set, based on the original modems from Hayes Microcomputer Products, Inc. Every command starts with the letters AT, for ATtention. The most common commands include ATDT (dial a number), ATA (manually answer the phone), ATZ (reset modem), ATS0=0 (disable auto-answer), and ATH (hang up the phone).

HD

See DSHD.

high-speed modem

A modem operating at speeds from 9,600 to 28,800 bits per second.

HOME key

This key is supposed to move the cursor to the upper-left corner of the screen. In truth, it does a number of different things, depending on the program. Often it moves the cursor to the beginning of the current line.

IBM-compatible PC

A computer that has been built to be compatible with the industry standard IBM PC. All IBM-compatible PCs should be able to run the same software.

icons

Small on-screen pictorial representations of programs and documents. Used in GUIs.

IDE (integrated drive electronics)

A disk drive with its own controller electronics built in to save space and money.

Industry Standard Architecture

See ISA.

information superhighway

The over-hyped concept of a cross-country telecommunications infrastructure built by business and government for the use of all the people. Sometimes considered synonymous with the Internet.

init string

A list of letters and numbers sent to a modem to set it up for a telecommunication session. Usually begins with AT (see Hayes-compatible modems) and ends with a carriage return.

inkjet printer

A printer that sprays a fine jet of liquid ink on the page. Inkjet printers are inexpensive, but produce high-quality output.

input

Verb: To enter data into the computer. Noun: the data that is being entered into the computer

INSERT key

A key that in many instances is a "toggle." (This means that if you press the key it will turn a function on or off.) The Insert key will turn the insert mode on or off. If you turn off the insert mode and begin to type, you will write over existing text. With the insert mode on you would place new text between existing text.

integrated circuit (IC)

A tiny complex of electronic components and their connections that is produced in or on a slice of material (such as silicon). A single IC can hold many electronic elements. Also called a chip.

Integrated Services Digital Network

See ISDN.

Intel

A major manufacturer of integrated circuits used in computers. Intel makes the 8086 family of microprocessors and its derivatives: the 8088, 80286, 80386SX and DX, and 80486SX and DX, and Pentium. These are the chips used in the IBM PC family of computers.

interactive
Computer software that provides many opportunities for user input.

interlaced and noninterlaced scanning
Two monitor schemes with which to paint an image on the screen. Interlaced scanning takes two passes, painting every other line on the first pass and filling in the rest of the lines on the second pass. Noninterlaced scanning paints all the lines in one pass and then paints an entirely new frame. Noninterlaced scanning is preferable because it reduces screen flicker, but it's more expensive.

Internet
An interconnected network of three million computer systems in 70 countries. Many of the participating computer systems offer free file transfers, e-mail, and even computing time.

Internet Service Provider
See ISP.

interrupt conflict
When two or more devices use the same IRQ a conflict occurs that can cause the devices to stop working or work erratically.

IRQ (interrupt request)
A request for attention from a peripheral device to the CPU. Setting two peripherals to the same IRQ is a cause of hair pulling among desktop PC users.

ISA (Industry Standard Architecture)
Computers using the same bus structure and add-in cards as the IBM PC, XT, and AT.

ISDN (Integrated Services Digital Network)
An international standard for digital telecommunications. ISDN offers two 64 kbps voice and data channels and one 16 Kbps control channel.

ISP (Internet Service Provider)
A company that sells connections to the Internet for both individuals and businesses.

jaggies
The stair-step appearance of diagonal lines on low resolution displays.

joystick

A device for controlling computer games. Joysticks usually have a single upright stick used for moving the pointer, and one or more buttons for clicking or firing.

jumpers

Simple metal connectors used to configure circuit boards. When the pins are connected the jumper is closed.

kbps (kilobits per second)

The unit of measure for modem speeds, equal to 1,024 bits per second.

kilo

One thousand, but in computers, it's typically 1,024 (2 to the tenth power).

kilobyte

1,024 bytes. Sometimes abbreviated as k (lowercase), K-byte, K, or KB for kilobyte and kb for kilobit (1,024 bits). When in doubt about whether an abbreviation refers to kilobytes or kilobits, it's probably kilobytes, with these exceptions: the speed of a modem (as in 2.4 kilobits per second) and the transfer rate of a floppy disk (as in 500 kilobits per second).

LAN (local area network)

A small to moderate-sized network in which communications are usually confined to a relatively small area, such as a single building or campus.

laptop

A small, portable computer. Usually 10 pounds or less.

laser printers.

High-quality printers that use photocopier technology to put a high-resolution image on plain paper.

lithium ion

A modern technology for rechargeable batteries that offers longer life.

local bus

A special high-speed connection between the CPU, memory, and peripherals that by-passes the slow ISA bus. Chiefly used to speed up video displays.

log on or in; log off or out

The process of connecting or disconnecting your computer to another system by modem.

LPT port (line printer port)

The connector on the back of PC used for connecting a printer. Sometimes called the parallel port.

Macintosh

An easy-to-use personal computer line made by Apple Computer, Inc.

macro language

A computer program that records keystrokes and mouse clicks and then plays them back on demand. More sophisticated macro languages allow the user to modify these scripts and add other commands.

MB

1,048,576 bytes (1,024 times 1,024). Used to describe the total capacity of a hard or floppy disk or the total amount of RAM. Sometimes abbreviated as Mb, M, MB, or meg for megabyte; and Mb, M-bit, or Mbit for megabit.

mean time between failure

See MTBF.

mega

One million, but with computers it typically means 1,048,576 (1,024 times 1,024).

megabyte

See MB.

megahertz

See mHz.

memory

A device that stores data in a computer. Internal memories are very fast and are either read/write random-access memory (RAM) or read-only memory (ROM). Bulk storage devices are either fixed disk, floppy disk, tape, or optical memories; these hold large amounts of data, but are slower to access than internal memories.

memory manager

A program for PCs that optimizes memory use to make more memory available to programs that need it.

mHz (megahertz)

One million cycles per second, typically used in reference to a computer's clock rate.

microprocessor

An integrated circuit (IC) that communicates, controls, and executes machine language instructions.

MIDI (musical instrument digital interface)

A standard for hooking up musical instruments to computers, and for storing musical scores on a computer.

modem

A combination of the words *modulate* and *demodulate*. A device that allows a computer to communicate with another computer over telephone lines.

monitor

Your computer's display.

motherboard

The main circuit board of a personal computer. The motherboard is home to the computer's CPU, RAM, ROM, and slots for adapter cards.

Motorola

A major chip manufacturer known for the 68000 family used in Apple Macintosh computers (68000, 68020, 68030, and 68040) and for the PowerPC chip (the 601, 603, 604, and 620) used in computers from Apple, IBM, and others.

mouse

A device used to control the onscreen cursor in programs with graphical user interfaces. As the mouse is moved on the desk, the pointer on the screen moves correspondingly.

MPC Level II

Microsoft's standard for multimedia hardware. An MPC-II computer has at minimum a 486SX-25 CPU, 4MB RAM, 160MB hard disk, VGA display with 65,000 colors at 640 × 480, a 16-bit sound card with MISI, and a double speed CD-ROM. Many newer multimedia titles require an MPC-II compliant machine.

MPEG (Motion Picture Experts Group)

A standard for compressed video. MPEG I provides VCR quality video. MPEG II will offer broadcast quality video.

MPR II

The stringent Swedish government standard for maximum radiation emmissions from a video display.

MS-DOS (Microsoft Disk Operating System)

The most popular operating system for IBM PCs and compatibles. Required to run Windows.

MTBF (mean time between failures)

How long your computer or other equipment runs before it breaks, based on component testing.

multimedia

The presentation of information on a computer using sound, graphics, animation, video, and text.

multitask

Running two or more programs at the same time. Special operating system software is required to multitask. Unix, Windows, Macintosh, and OS/2 are all multitasking operating systems.

Musical Instrument Digital Interface

See MIDI.

network

A continuing connection between two or more computers that facilitates sharing files and resources.

newsgroups

Internet discussion groups in which messages on specific topics and their replies are publically posted. There are over 12,000 newsgroups, each covering a different topic.

nickel cadmium

The most common rechargeable battery technology, suffers from short battery life, and the "memory effect" which prevents complete recharging if the battery isn't fully discharged.

nickel hydride (NIHM)

A more sophisticated rechargeable battery technology that doesn't suffer from the memory effect (see nickel cadmium).

NIMH

See nickel hydride.

notebook

A small portable computer that weighs between four and seven pounds.

NuBus

A bus architecture developed at MIT and adapted by Apple for its Macintosh computers.

NUMLOCK key

Press this key to force the numeric keypad to only type numbers.

OCR software (optical character recognition)

Software that can "read" the text from the printed page and turn it into editable computer text. Useful for copying documents into the computer.

office suite

A bundle of major office applications from a single vendor. Typically includes stand-alone word processor, spreadsheet, presentation graphics, and database applications.

online service

A company that provides a wide variety of information and entertainment on computers that you can access with a modem.

online/offline

When connected to another computer via modem and telephone lines, a modem is said to be online. When disconnected, it is offline.

operating system

A set of programs residing in ROM and/or on disk that controls communications between components of the computer and the programs run by the computer. MS-DOS is an operating system.

optical character recognition software

See OCR.

OS/2 (Operating System/2)

An operating system developed by IBM and Microsoft for use with Intel's microprocessors. Unlike its predecessor, DOS, OS/2 is a multitasking operating system. This means many programs can run on it at the same time.

Page Up/Page Down

Move the cursor up or down 25 lines, usually a full page. In telecommunications programs these keys are used to begin to send or to get ready to receive files.

palette

The set of colors that a computer can display.

parallel port

A port that transmits or receives 8 bits (1 byte) of data at a time between the computer and external devices. Mainly used by printers. LPT1 is a parallel port, for example.

passive matrix

A kind of liquid crystal display (LCD) often used in laptops. It's less expensive than active matrix, but not as crisp. Colors are more washed out.

pause key

Press this key to stop the screen display in DOS. Press it again to continue.

PC (personal computer)

Sometimes used generically to represent all inexpensive computers. More often used to describe IBM PC compatible personal computers.

PC Card

A credit-card sized peripheral device for use in laptop computers. PC Card devices include modems, network cards, memory, and even hard disks.

PCI Bus (peripheral component interconnect)

A high-speed local bus specification created by Intel and found most often on Pentium systems. Apple will begin building PCI-based Power Mac computers in 1995.

PCMCIA

See PC Card.

peripheral

A device that performs a function and is external to the system board. Peripherals include displays, disk drives, and printers.

phosphor

The material used to coat the inside of your CRT screen. It glows when struck by electrons.

PIM (personal information manager)

A program that manages a person's collection of personal information, keeping track of notes, memos, time planning, telephone numbers, and addresses.

pirate software

The act of making or distributing an unauthorized copy of a copyrighted software product for financial gain. In most countries such an act is prohibited by law.

pixel

A pixel is the smallest building block of an on-screen image. On a color monitor screen, each pixel is made of one or more triads (red, green, and blue). Resolution is usually expressed in terms of the number of pixels that fit within the width and height of a complete on-screen image. In VGA, the resolution is 640 by 480 pixels; in SuperVGA, it is 800 by 600 pixels.

plotter

A printer that draws with pens. Used for creating blue prints, and other large designs.

port

The interface between the microprocessor and peripheral devices.

POST (power on self-test)

The test sequence that begins when your computer is turned on.

power on self-test

See POST.

power supply

The converter that turns AC electrical current into the DC your computer uses. The power supply is located within the case on desktop computers, and usually outside the case on laptops.

Print Screen key

In DOS you can press this key to print the entire screen. If a printer is not connected, or not turned on, your computer will pause for a minute or two while trying to print.

processor cache

High-speed memory that is used to store instructions that have been recently executed by the CPU. These instructions will be quickly available should the CPU require them again. Since this often happens, a processor cache can speed up your computer considerably.

programming language

Any artificial language that can be used to define a sequence of instructions that can ultimately be processed and executed by the computer.

protocol

Rules governing communications, including flow control (start-stop), error detection or correction, and parameters (data bits, stop bits, parity). If they use the same protocols, products from different vendors can communicate.

QIC (quarter-inch cartridge)

A common format used for backup tapes.

QWERTY

The keyboard arrangement on computers and typewriters, after the Q-W-E-R-T-Y layout of the top row of the alphabet keys.

RAM (random access memory)

Also known as read-write memory; the memory used to execute application programs.

RAM disk

A part of RAM that is used as a disk. Since RAM is so much faster than a hard disk, a RAM disk can be used to speed things up. But a RAM disk is dangerous for storing data because the contents are lost if the computer crashes or if power is turned off. Most users with extra RAM prefer to use it for a disk cache rather than as a RAM disk.

random access memory

See RAM.

resolution

The number of dots and lines displayed on a computer screen. A VGA display, for example, is 640 dots wide and 480 lines high. The higher the resolution on a given screen, the smaller the dots.

RETURN key

See ENTER key.

RGB (red, green, blue)

The triad, the three colors, that make up one pixel of a color monitor. All other colors can be made from these three.

ROM (read-only memory)

The memory chip(s) that permanently store computer information and instructions. Your computer's BIOS (basic input/output system) information is stored in a ROM chip. Some laptops even have the operating system (DOS) in ROM.

RSI

See carpal tunnel syndrome.

sample

A digitized piece of sound. When recording sound on your computer, the higher the sampling rate, the higher quality the sound.

scalable fonts

Fonts that can be displayed or printed at any size.

scanner

A peripheral device that digitizes documents or pictures for storage on the computer.

Scroll Lock key

A vestigial key from the early days of the PC. Very few programs use the Scroll Lock key.

SCSI (small computer system interface)

An interface for connecting peripheral devices to your computer. It allows up to seven devices to be connected to a single adapter.

serial port

The "male" connector (usually DB-9 or DB-25) on the back of your computer. It sends out data one bit at a time. It is used by modems and, in years past, for daisy-wheel and other printers. The other port on your computer is the parallel port, which is a "female" connector. It is used for printers, backup systems, and mini-networking (LANs). *See also* COM port.

shareware

Copyrighted software that is distributed free of charge but is usually accompanied by a request for a small payment from satisfied users to cover costs and registration for documentation and program updates. These programs range from fully functional programs to ones having only limited features.

shock-mounted

A hard drive or other device that has been specially fitted to resist damage from being dropped.

silicon

The element used as the base for all integrated circuits.

SIMM (single inline memory modules)

A circuit board that holds several RAM chips. Used for adding memory to your mother board.

single inline memory modules

See SIMM.

slot

A socket for adding adapter cards to your computer.

small computer systems interface

See SCSI.

Q/A

smiley

Abbreviations commonly used online and in e-mail to express feelings. The first smiley was :-) (Turn your head sideways to see the face.)

software

The programs you run on your computer. Software includes programming tools, operating systems, and application programs like electronic spreadsheets and word processors.

sound card

An adapter card used to add sound record and playback to IBM PC compatibles.

Sound Blaster

The most popular line of sound cards, made by Creative Labs. Also a de facto standard for sound card compatibility.

spreadsheet

An application commonly used for budgets, forecasting, and other finance-related tasks. Data and formulas to calculate those data are entered into ledger-like forms (spreadsheets or worksheets) for analysis, tracking, planning, and evaluation of impacts on economic strategy.

street price

The real or typical selling price of computers, hardware, and software. Most computers sell for about 25 percent below list price. Software may be discounted even more.

subdirectory

Like folders (*See* folders), subdirectories (or directories) are used to organize files on a disk. Subdirectories may contain either files or other subdirectories.

Super VGA

An enhanced graphics standard for IBM PC compatibles. Specifies 256 colors at a resolution of 800 by 600.

surge protector

A device that protects your computer from excessive voltage from your outlet.

swap file

> A file used to simulate RAM. When your system runs low on memory, some operating systems will let you use disk space instead.

SX

> A designation Intel adds to the names of its 386 and 486 chips. On a 386 the SX means it has a 16-bit data path. On a 486 it means that the chip's built-in math co-processor has been disabled. For users that don't require the more advanced features, SX chips can be a good deal.

SysReq (system request key)

> The seldom-used key used to get attention from another computer.

tablet

> *See* drawing tablet.

tape drive

> A peripheral used for backing up the contents of your hard disk to tape. Combines high capacity with slow speed. Good for backing up large disks overnight.

technical support

> Help in installing or operating hardware or software, usually from the manufacturer. Some tech support is free. Some companies charge.

telecommunication

> Using your computer to communicate with another computer via telephone lines and your modem.

terminal emulator

> A program that turns your computer into a simple terminal, like the kind they use to check you in at the airport.

TrueType

> A scalable font technology jointly developed by Microsoft and Apple and used in both Windows and Macintosh computers. Lets you print any font at any size.

typeface

> A family of fonts. Common typefaces are Arial, Times Roman, and Courier.

UART (universal asynchronous receiver transmitter)
The circuit that controls the serial port, converting bytes to bits and bits to bytes, and adding and stripping start and stop bits. Buying tip: Look for a computer with a 16550A or 16550AF UART instead of the older, slower 16450 or 8250 UARTs if you're planning to do high-speed data communications.

uniform resource locator
See URL.

URL (uniform resource locator)
The addresses used to locate information on the Internet.

Usenet newsgroups
See newsgroups.

V.
The CCITT international communications standards, pronounced "vee-dot." Various V. standards cover speed (modulation), error correction, data compression, and signaling characteristics.

V.22
1,200 bps modem speed, about 120 characters per second. Most 1,200 bps communication in the United States uses the Bell 212A standard instead. Above 1,200 bps, all standards are the same around the world.

V.22*bis*
2,400 bps modem speed.

V.29
9,600 bps data communications (also 4,800 and 7,200) used by Group III fax machines and PC fax modems. Fax modems, at least of the same brand, can exchange nonfax data at 9,600 bps, usually in half-duplex mode (one way at a time).

V.32
9,600 bps data communications (also 4,800). Most but not all 9,600 bps modems support V.32 or V.32*bis*.

V.32*bis*
A follow-up to V.32 that allows 14,400 bps (also 4,800, 7,200, 9,600, and 12,000) data communications. V.29 is 9,600 bps, but it can't talk to V.32.

V.32*ter*

19,200 bps. Successor to V.32*bis*. (*ter* is Latin for third). This standard was a short-lived interim solution. You should avoid it and go with either V.32*bis* or V.34.

V.34

28,800 bps. This standard was just ratified in late 1994. These super-high speed modems should become common in the next few years. They represent the highest speed that can be transmitted over standard voice telephone lines.

V.42

An error correction standard. Most modern modems have this built-in to reduce the number of data errors.

V.42*bis*

Emerging data-compression standard, better than MNP 5 data compression because it compresses data up to 4:1 (versus 2:1). Includes the V.42 error-control standard, so even if a modem is listed as having V.42*bis* but not V.42, it has both. Buying caution: A "V.42*bis*-compatible" modem may only have MNP 5, not LAPM; a "V.42*bis*-compliant" modem should have both. Ask before you buy.

V.FAST

A non-standard 28,800 bps modem. Avoid these like the plague, they don't work with hardly anything! If you've got one, upgrade it to V.34 as quickly as you can.

VESA (Video Electronics Standards Association)

A consortium of manufacturers formed to establish and maintain industry-wide standards for video cards and monitors. VESA is responsible for establishing the Super VGA recommendations that many manufacturers follow today.

VGA

IBM's third (1987) and current mainstream graphics standard, capable of 640-by-480-pixel resolution at 16 colors or gray shades. Most VGA cards can support 256 colors.

Video Electronics Standards Association

See VESA.

virtual memory

See swap file.

virus

A small program that is designed to invade your computer and modify its operation without your knowledge. Most viruses are harmful.

VL-Bus

VESA's local bus standard. This is the one to get if you're buying a 486-based PC.

VRAM (video random-access memory)

Special-purpose RAM for video cards.

wave table synthesis

A high quality music reproduction technique that uses samples from real instruments instead of synthesized sounds to play back music.

window

An area of a screen that displays information. Some programs support several windows that can be viewed simultaneously or sequentially.

Windows

The best-selling operating system in the world. This Microsoft GUI runs on IBM PC compatibles.

Windows accelerator card

An adapter card that's optimized for running Windows software. Works much faster as long as you're using Windows.

word processing

A program that's designed for the creation and editing of text documents.

Works

Single programs that offer complete word processor, database, spreadsheet, and graphics functions.

write protection

Keeping a file or disk from being written over or deleted. 3½-inch floppy disks use a sliding write-protect tab in the lower-left corner to keep the computer from writing to the disk. When the tab is open, the disk is write-protected.

WYSIWYG (What You See Is What You Get)

A screen display that closely matches the printed output.

More Help from Ziff-Davis Press

Ziff-Davis Press offers a diverse selection of books and CD-ROMs to help computer users—both novices and old hands—get the most from their systems. Here are some products that are guaranteed to help you with your computing needs. To order these books or to receive a free Ziff-Davis Press catalog, call 1-800-688-0448.

General Guides for Mac and PC Users

How to Use Your Computer   It's out of the box. Now what? This guide takes it from the top. You'll find a PC anatomy lesson; clear explanations of DOS, Windows, and memory; advice on getting started with telecommunication; and more.

The Mac Almanac   Written for every Mac enthusiast or wannabe, this is an entertaining and informative compendium of all things Mac. You'll find techniques and tricks about the system, hardware and software, and memory management, as well as shameless Mac trivia and anecdotes. Guaranteed to make you laugh out loud as you learn.

Help with Learning Applications

The How to Use Series

This series' easy-to-read explanations and pleasing graphics are perfect for beginners. You'll find "Try It" sections that help you practice important techniques and features and "Tip Sheets" with practical advice and troubleshooting hints.

- ➤ *How to Use Word 6.0*
- ➤ *How to Use Ami Pro 4.0*
- ➤ *How to Use WordPerfect 6.1 for Windows*
- ➤ *How to Use Windows 95*
- ➤ *How to Use Microsoft Excel*
- ➤ *How to Use Microsoft Access*
- ➤ *How to Use 1-2-3 5.0*

The PC Learning Labs Series

The techniques in these best-selling books have been tested on thousands of first-time users in the classrooms of PC Learning Labs, one of the largest single-site training centers in the world. Books in this series feature a book/disk learning system with easy-to-follow practice sessions and helpful reference information that will come in handy even after you learn the program.

- ➤ *PC Learning Labs Teaches FoxPro*
- ➤ *PC Learning Labs Teaches Microsoft Access*

Q/A

➤ *PC Learning Labs Teaches Microsoft Office*

➤ *PC Learning Labs Teaches Word 6.0 for Windows*

➤ *PC Learning Labs Teaches Excel 5.0 for Windows*

➤ *PC Learning Labs Teaches 1-2-3 5.0 for Windows*

➤ *PC Learning Labs Teaches Windows 95*

➤ *PC Learning Labs Teaches Ami Pro 4.0*

➤ *PC Learning Labs Teaches WordPerfect (for DOS and Windows)*

➤ *PC Learning Labs Teaches DOS 6*

Incorporating Your Computer into Your Life with the Total Planning Series

Millions of people are taking the computer beyond the workplace and into their personal lives. Each *Total Planning* book presents a comprehensive strategy that any computer user can follow to organize and improve an important area of living.

➤ *SMART TRAVEL: Total Planning on Your Computer*

➤ *YOUR HEALTH: Total Healthcare Planning*

➤ *YOUR MONEY: Total Financial Planning*

➤ *YOUR CHILD'S EDUCATION: Total Planning on Your Computer*

➤ *HOME IMPROVEMENT: Total Planning on Your Computer*

➤ *YOUR NEW OFFICE: Total Planning for Telecommuters*

➤ *YOUR ROOTS: Total Genealogy Planning on Your Computer*

Help with Navigating the Information Highway

These books can help you hook up with the Internet, dial up to an online service, or just learn more about the quickly evolving world of cyberspace.

How to Connect   The artfully written and colorfully illustrated road map for first-time travelers on the information highway. Includes explanations of how to

Q/A

choose and install a modem, how to make your first connection, and how to pick the best online services and subscribe to them.

net.talk   The definitive dictionary of the acronyms and emoticons so popular with online communicators.

Futurekids: The Internet Expedition   This 64-page full-color comic book for readers 8 and older was produced by Futurekids, a leading operator of hands-on computer learning centers for children.

Cybersource '95   A freewheeling look at the people, services, and products that make up the computer industry. Includes essays and reviews from the world's most well-respected industry commentators.

Traveler's Guide to the Information Highway   In this innovative guide in the spirit of the travel book, real maps point the way to online services and all that they offer. Filled with tips, shortcuts, and traveler's advisories.

Guides for the online beginner from the bestselling *How to Use* series.

➤ *How to Use America Online*

➤ *How to Use Prodigy*

➤ *How to Use the Internet*

Atlas to the World Wide Web   A directory to the gold mine of services available from the Internet's Web, this atlas describes over 1,000 Web sites, ranging from aeronautics to zoology.

Multimedia

How Computers Work   This 1994 gold-medal winner in the Consumer Enrichment—Computer Sciences category of the New York Festivals has a "hot" environment with a clickable interface, tons of animation, and crisp graphics. Includes fast-paced tours showing how a CD-ROM stores so much information, how a monitor displays color, and how a disk drive works.

INDEX

Ziff-Davis Press Survey of Readers

Please help us in our effort to produce the best books on personal computing.
For your assistance, we would be pleased to send you a FREE catalog
featuring the complete line of Ziff-Davis Press books.

1. How did you first learn about this book?

Recommended by a friend . . . . ☐ -1 (5)

Recommended by store personnel . . . . ☐ -2

Saw in Ziff-Davis Press catalog . . . . ☐ -3

Received advertisement in the mail . . . . ☐ -4

Saw the book on bookshelf at store . . . . ☐ -5

Read book review in: _____ ☐ -6

Saw an advertisement in: _____ ☐ -7

Other (Please specify): _____ ☐ -8

2. Which THREE of the following factors most influenced your decision to purchase this book? (Please check up to THREE.)

Front or back cover information on book . . . ☐ -1 (6)

Logo of magazine affiliated with book . . . . . ☐ -2

Special approach to the content . . . . ☐ -3

Completeness of content . . . . ☐ -4

Author's reputation. ☐ -5

Publisher's reputation . . . . ☐ -6

Book cover design or layout . . . . ☐ -7

Index or table of contents of book . . . . ☐ -8

Price of book . . . . ☐ -9

Special effects, graphics, illustrations . . . . . . ☐ -0

Other (Please specify): _____ ☐ -x

3. How many computer books have you purchased in the last six months? _____ (7-10)

4. On a scale of 1 to 5, where 5 is excellent, 4 is above average, 3 is average, 2 is below average, and 1 is poor, please rate each of the following aspects of this book below. (Please circle your answer.)

Depth/completeness of coverage	5	4	3	2	1	(11)
Organization of material	5	4	3	2	1	(12)
Ease of finding topic	5	4	3	2	1	(13)
Special features/time saving tips	5	4	3	2	1	(14)
Appropriate level of writing	5	4	3	2	1	(15)
Usefulness of table of contents	5	4	3	2	1	(16)
Usefulness of index	5	4	3	2	1	(17)
Usefulness of accompanying disk	5	4	3	2	1	(18)
Usefulness of illustrations/graphics	5	4	3	2	1	(19)
Cover design and attractiveness	5	4	3	2	1	(20)
Overall design and layout of book	5	4	3	2	1	(21)
Overall satisfaction with book	5	4	3	2	1	(22)

5. Which of the following computer publications do you read regularly; that is, 3 out of 4 issues?

Byte . . . . ☐ -1 (23)

Computer Shopper . . . . ☐ -2

Home Office Computing . . . . ☐ -3

Dr. Dobb's Journal . . . . ☐ -4

LAN Magazine . . . . ☐ -5

MacWEEK . . . . ☐ -6

MacUser . . . . ☐ -7

PC Computing . . . . ☐ -8

PC Magazine . . . . ☐ -9

PC WEEK . . . . ☐ -0

Windows Sources . . . . ☐ -x

Other (Please specify): _____ ☐ -y

Please turn page.

6. What is your level of experience with personal computers? With the subject of this book?

	With PCs	With subject of book
Beginner	☐ -1 (24)	☐ -1 (25)
Intermediate	☐ -2	☐ -2
Advanced	☐ -3	☐ -3

7. Which of the following best describes your job title?

Officer (CEO/President/VP/owner)........ ☐ -1 (26)
Director/head......................... ☐ -2
Manager/supervisor.................... ☐ -3
Administration/staff.................. ☐ -4
Teacher/educator/trainer.............. ☐ -5
Lawyer/doctor/medical professional....... ☐ -6
Engineer/technician................... ☐ -7
Consultant........................... ☐ -8
Not employed/student/retired............ ☐ -9
Other (Please specify): _____ ☐ -0

8. What is your age?

Under 20............................ ☐ -1 (27)
21-29............................... ☐ -2
30-39............................... ☐ -3
40-49............................... ☐ -4
50-59............................... ☐ -5
60 or over.......................... ☐ -6

9. Are you:

Male................................ ☐ -1 (28)
Female.............................. ☐ -2

Thank you for your assistance with this important information! Please write your address below to receive our free catalog.

Name: _____

Address: _____

City/State/Zip: _____

Fold here to mail.

3393-16-19

_____

_____

_____